ROLAND BARTHES

'While not always distorting the truth about a given cultural phenomenon, to control and master it all too often deadens its impact, arresting
its creative effects. Ironically, however, in controlling and mastering
Roland Barthes's dauntingly variegated oeuvre, in bringing coherence
to its wilful contradictions, the author of this volume liberates that
work, making it available as one of the best examples of free critical
thinking that the twentieth century had to offer.'
       Robert Harvey, *State University of New York at Stony Brook*

Roland Barthes is a central figure in the study of language, literature,
culture and the media, both as innovator and guide. This book prepares
readers for their first encounter with his crucial writings on some of
the most important theoretical debates of the twentieth century,
including:

* Existentialism and Marxism
* semiology, or the 'language of signs'
* structuralism and narrative analysis
* post-structuralism, deconstruction and 'the death of the author'
* theories of the text and intertextuality.

   In exploring Barthes's most influential ideas and their impact,
Graham Allen traces his engagement with other key thinkers such as
Jean-Paul Sartre, Ferdinand de Saussure, Jacques Derrida and Julia
Kristeva. He concludes with a guide to easily available translations of
key texts by Barthes and offers invaluable advice on further reading.
   The in-depth understanding of Barthes offered by this guide is essen-
tial to anyone reading contemporary critical theory.

Graham Allen is Senior Lecturer in English at University College,
Cork. He is the author of *Intertextuality* in Routledge's New Critical
Idiom series and has published widely on literary theory and
Romanticism.

ROUTLEDGE CRITICAL THINKERS

Series Editor: Robert Eaglestone, Royal Holloway, University of London

Routledge Critical Thinkers is a series of accessible introductions to key figures in contemporary critical thought.

With a unique focus on historical and intellectual contexts, each volume examines a key theorist's:

- significance
- motivation
- key ideas and their sources
- impact on other thinkers

Concluding with extensively annotated guides to further reading, *Routledge Critical Thinkers* are the student's passport to today's most exciting critical thought.

Already available:
Roland Barthes by Graham Allen
Jean Baudrillard by Richard J. Lane
Maurice Blanchot by Ullrich Haase and William Large
Judith Butler by Sara Salih
Gilles Deleuze by Claire Colebrook
Jacques Derrida by Nicholas Royle
Michel Foucault by Sara Mills
Sigmund Freud by Pamela Thurschwell
Martin Heidegger by Timothy Clark
Fredric Jameson by Adam Roberts
Jean-François Lyotard by Simon Malpas
Paul de Man by Martin McQuillan
Friedrich Nietzsche by Lee Spinks
Paul Ricoeur by Karl Simms
Edward Said by Bill Ashcroft and Pal Ahluwalia
Gayatri Chakravorty Spivak by Stephen Morton

For further details on this series, see www.literature.routledge.com/rct

ROLAND BARTHES

Graham Allen

 Routledge
Taylor & Francis Group

LONDON AND NEW YORK

First published 2003
by Routledge
11 New Fetter Lane, London EC4P 4EE

Simultaneously published in the USA and Canada
by Routledge
29 West 35th Street, New York, NY 10001

Routledge is an imprint of the Taylor & Francis Group

© 2003 Graham Allen

Typeset in Perpetua by
Florence Production Ltd, Stoodleigh, Devon
Printed and bound in Great Britain by
TJ International, Padstow, Cornwall

British Library Cataloguing in Publication Data
A catalogue record for this book is available from the
British Library

Library of Congress Cataloging in Publication Data
Allen, Graham.
  Roland Barthes/Graham Allen.
    p. cm. – (Routledge critical thinkers)
  Includes bibliographical references and index.
  1. Barthes, Roland. I. Title. II. Series.
  P85.B33A79 2003
  410'.92 – dc21   2003002340

ISBN 0–415–26361–1 (hbk)
ISBN 0–415–26362-X (pbk)

CONTENTS

Series editor's preface   ix
Acknowledgements   xiii
List of abbreviations   xv

WHY BARTHES?   1

KEY IDEAS   7
1   Writing and Literature   9
2   Critical distance   25
3   Semiology   33
4   Structuralism   53
5   The death of the author   63
6   Textuality   79
7   Neutral writing: pleasure, violence and the novelistic   95
8   Music and photography   115
9   *Camera Lucida*: the impossible text   125

AFTER BARTHES   133

FURTHER READING   141

Works cited   155
Index   163

SERIES EDITOR'S PREFACE

The books in this series offer introductions to major critical thinkers who have influenced literary studies and the humanities. The *Routledge Critical Thinkers* series provides the books you can turn to first when a new name or concept appears in your studies.

Each book will equip you to approach a key thinker's original texts by explaining her or his key ideas, putting them into context and, perhaps most importantly, showing you why this thinker is considered to be significant. The emphasis is on concise, clearly written guides which do not presuppose a specialist knowledge. Although the focus is on particular figures, the series stresses that no critical thinker ever existed in a vacuum but, instead, emerged from a broader intellectual, cultural and social history. Finally, these books will act as a bridge between you and the thinker's original texts: not replacing them but rather complementing what she or he wrote.

These books are necessary for a number of reasons. In his 1997 autobiography, *Not Entitled*, the literary critic Frank Kermode wrote of a time in the 1960s:

> On beautiful summer lawns, young people lay together all night, recovering from their daytime exertions and listening to a troupe of Balinese musicians. Under their blankets or their sleeping bags, they would chat drowsily about the gurus of the time ... What they repeated was largely hearsay; hence my

lunchtime suggestion, quite impromptu, for a series of short, very cheap books
offering authoritative but intelligible introductions to such figures.

There is still a need for 'authoritative and intelligible introductions'.
But this series reflects a different world from the 1960s. New thinkers
have emerged and the reputations of others have risen and fallen, as
new research has developed. New methodologies and challenging ideas
have spread through arts and humanities. The study of literature is no
longer – if it ever was – simply the study and evaluation of poems,
novels and plays. It is also the study of ideas, issues, and difficulties
which arise in any literary text and in its interpretation. Other arts and
humanities subjects have changed in analogous ways.

With these changes, new problems have emerged. The ideas and
issues behind these radical changes in the humanities are often
presented without reference to wider contexts or as theories which
you can simply 'add on' to the texts you read. Certainly, there's nothing wrong with picking out selected ideas or using what comes to hand
– indeed, some thinkers have argued that this is, in fact, all we can
do. However, it is sometimes forgotten that each new idea comes from
the pattern and development of somebody's thought and it is important to study the range and context of their ideas. Against theories
'floating in space', the *Routledge Critical Thinkers* series places key
thinkers and their ideas firmly back in their contexts.

More than this, these books reflect the need to go back to the
thinker's own texts and ideas. Every interpretation of an idea, even
the most seemingly innocent one, offers its own 'spin', implicitly or
explicitly. To read only books on a thinker, rather than texts by that
thinker, is to deny yourself a chance of making up your own mind.
Sometimes what makes a significant figure's work hard to approach is
not so much its style or content as the feeling of not knowing where
to start. The purpose of these books is to give you a 'way in' by offering
an accessible overview of these thinkers' ideas and works and by
guiding your further reading, starting with each thinker's own texts.
To use a metaphor from the philosopher Ludwig Wittgenstein (1889–
1951), these books are ladders, to be thrown away after you have
climbed to the next level. Not only, then, do they equip you to
approach new ideas, but also they empower you, by leading you back
to the theorist's own texts and encouraging you to develop your own
informed opinions.

Finally, these books are necessary because, just as intellectual needs have changed, the education systems around the world – the contexts in which introductory books are usually read – have changed radically, too. What was suitable for the minority higher education system of the 1960s is not suitable for the larger, wider, more diverse, high technology education systems of the twenty-first century. These changes call not just for new, up-to-date, introductions but new methods of presentation. The presentational aspects of *Routledge Critical Thinkers* have been developed with today's students in mind.

Each book in the series has a similar structure. They begin with a section offering an overview of the life and ideas of each thinker and explain why she or he is important. The central section of each book discusses the thinker's key ideas, their context, evolution and reception. Each book concludes with a survey of the thinker's impact, outlining how their ideas have been taken up and developed by others. In addition, there is a detailed final section suggesting and describing books for further reading. This is not a 'tacked-on' section but an integral part of each volume. In the first part of this section you will find brief descriptions of the thinker's key works: following this, information on the most useful critical works and, in some cases, on relevant websites. This section will guide you in your reading, enabling you to follow your interests and develop your own projects. Throughout each book, references are given in what is known as the Harvard system (the author and the date of a work cited are given in the text and you can look up the full details in the bibliography at the back). This offers a lot of information in very little space. The books also explain technical terms and use boxes to describe events or ideas in more detail, away from the main emphasis of the discussion. Boxes are also used at times to highlight definitions of terms frequently used or coined by a thinker. In this way, the boxes serve as a kind of glossary, easily identified when flicking through the book.

The thinkers in the series are 'critical' for three reasons. First, they are examined in the light of subjects which involve criticism: principally literary studies or English and cultural studies, but also other disciplines which rely on the criticism of books, ideas, theories and unquestioned assumptions. Second, they are critical because studying their work will provide you with a 'tool kit' for your own informed critical reading and thought, which will make you critical. Third, these thinkers are critical because they are crucially important: they deal with ideas and questions which can overturn conventional understandings of the world, of texts, of everything we take for granted, leaving us with a deeper understanding of what we already knew and with new ideas.

No introduction can tell you everything. However, by offering a way into critical thinking, this series hopes to begin to engage you in an activity which is productive, constructive and potentially life-changing.

ACKNOWLEDGEMENTS

I would like to thank Bob Eaglestone, Talia Rogers, Liz Thompson and all the team at Routledge for their professionalism and assistance. The main part of this book was written during leave of absence granted to me by University College, Cork, for which I am grateful. My greatest debt, as ever, is to Bernie and to Dani and Chrissie: thank you ever so much for bearing with me during the writing of this book. I would like to thank Tony Henderson for making the beautiful table on which this book was written; Alex Davis for providing me with more books than he is aware of lending; Paul Hegarty for all the chats, authentic advice and astonishingly precise reading, more inspiration than he is aware of, and, of course, for sharing a wonderful season; Ann Fitz for her infinite patience and her priceless friendship; Martin McHenry and the boys for their unprecedented awareness and, of course, their construction skills; Eibhéar Walshe for significant conversations about Barthes and other matters in Rome and in Cork; Malcolm Garrard for his gift of hearing what is in my head and allowing me to hear what is in his; Roy Sellars for being a comrade-in-arms and an inspiring friend; Nora Crook and Pam Morris for believing in me, for the gift of their time, and for giving me examples, as people and as academics, to attempt to emulate.

ABBREVIATIONS

Almost all of Barthes's works are available in English translation and these are abbreviated in the study as follows:

BSW — *Barthes: Selected Writings* (1982)
CE — *Critical Essays* (1972)
CL — *Camera Lucida: Reflections on Photography* (1981)
CT — *Criticism and Truth* (1987)
ESe — *Elements of Semiology* (1984)
ESi — *Empire of Signs* (1982)
ET — *The Eiffel Tower and Other Mythologies* (1979)
FS — *The Fashion System* (1983)
GV — *The Grain of the Voice: Interviews, 1962–1980* (1985)
IMT — *Image-Music-Text* (1977)
In — *Incidents* (1992)
LD — *A Lover's Discourse: Fragments* (1978)
M — *Michelet* (1987)
MY — *Mythologies* (1972)
NCE — *New Critical Essays* (1980)
OR — *On Racine* (1964)
PT — *The Pleasure of the Text* (1975)
RB — *Roland Barthes by Roland Barthes* (1977)
Res — 'Responses: Interview with *Tel Quel*' (1998)

RF   *The Responsibility of Forms* (1985)
RL   *The Rustle of Language* (1986)
SC   *The Semiotic Challenge* (1988)
SFL   *Sade/Fourier/Loyola* (1976)
SW   *Sollers Writer* (1987)
S/Z   *S/Z* (1974)
TT   'Theory of the Text' (1981)
WDZ   *Writing Degree Zero* (1984)

WHY BARTHES?

Roland Barthes is a crucial figure in modern literary and cultural theory. His work has been influential in a wide variety of theoretical trends and practices, including structuralism, semiology, post-structuralism, cultural studies and psychoanalytical literary criticism. Barthes is one of a handful of writers who can be said to have established the foundations for modern literary and cultural theory. To understand theory today one must come to know about and engage with his work.

Barthes is famous for many things: for announcing the 'death of the author'; for articulating the theory and practice of intertextuality; for promoting the study of cultural sign-systems such as we find in advertisements, the design of cars and buildings, the fashions we annually consume. A popular theorist read by many people outside as well as inside university departments and courses, it is Barthes who stands behind many of the most commonly recognized contemporary theories about literature, art and cultural life. Most students within the arts and the social sciences have been influenced by Barthes's ideas before they have read a single word of his writings.

BARTHES'S CAREER

Born in Cherbourg on 12 November 1915, Barthes was the son of Louis Barthes and Henriette Binger. Louis Barthes, a naval officer, died in action during the First World War before Barthes's first birthday. Barthes's early life was spent in Bayonne with his mother, his paternal grandmother, Berthe Barthes, and his aunt Alice, a piano teacher who inspired Barthes's life-long love of music. Although he moved to Paris with his mother in 1924, Bayonne, near the south-western border between France and Spain, remained an important place of return for Barthes throughout his life. Louis-Jean Calvet, Barthes's biographer, puts it this way: 'He always felt that he was Basque or Gascon, never Parisian, and still less, of course, Norman' (Calvet 1994: 12). Barthes's early manhood was dominated by two interrelated things: his obvious brilliance and promise as a student and, from 1934 onwards, ill health. From 1934 to 1947 Barthes suffered from repeated breakdowns in his health due to pulmonary tuberculosis, a disease which required lengthy treatment in isolated sanitoria. Tuberculosis meant the constant disruption of Barthes's studies. Institutionalized for long periods of time, Barthes was unable to complete the prestigious agrégation examinations which allow French scholars to gain posts in the traditional universities. As a consequence, Barthes's career as a professional academic is not the smooth and steady one we might imagine for such an internationally famous author. From the late 1940s to the early 1960s Barthes took up various short-term teaching and research posts in Romania and Egypt, and at a number of institutions in Paris. It was only in 1962 that Barthes's career began to gain stability in terms of permanent employment and academic recognition, when he was appointed Director of Studies at the École Prâtique des Hautes Études (EPHE). Barthes was finally received into the established realms of the French academy in 1976 when he was appointed Chair of Literary Semiology at the Collège de France. It should be noted that while the Collège de France is a far older, and in many senses more venerable, institution than the EPHE, both fall outside of the degree-awarding university sector. Both institutions are dedicated to postgraduate teaching and to the most innovative forms of research. Barthes's academic career, therefore, was conducted outside of the major degree-awarding institutions but within the environments of pure research. It would be a mistake, therefore, to view Barthes's ill health as a young man as the only determining factor in the ultimate shape of his academic career. As Barthes made clear, his career path was also oriented by a purposeful avoidance of power in the shape of degree-awarding universities such as the Sorbonne.

Barthes's acceptance of the Chair of Literary Semiology in the Collège de France is usually seen as a late acknowledgement of his by then pre-eminent position within French academic and intellectual culture. This acknowledgement came, however, with reservations on both sides. In the lecture given on the event of his inauguration Barthes speaks of himself as a 'patently impure fellow' entering, by implication without valid credentials, into 'an establishment where science, scholarship, rigor, and disciplined invention reign' (BSW: 458). Evidently concerned that his election to the Collège de France might associate him with things he had fought against all his writing life (power, the establishment, ideological norms, traditional values), Barthes's uneasiness seems also to have been shared by those who sponsored his election. Calvet, for example, cites a portion of Michel Foucault's report in favour of Barthes's election. Here Foucault describes Barthes's work as 'trendy' and associates it with 'fashions, enthusiasms, fads, or even exaggerations' of the moment. Foucault also states, however, that Barthes's work reveals 'the existence of more deep-rooted and fertile cultural phenomena'. He adds: 'These voices, these few voices heard today outside the universities, do they not form part of contemporary history? And should we not welcome them among us?' (Calvet 1994: 212–13). Foucault's description, no doubt, is concerned as much with himself as it is with Barthes. His positioning of Barthes in terms of a voice 'heard . . . outside the universities' is a telling and accurate one nonetheless.

THEORY: SPEAKING FROM SOMEWHERE ELSE

Roland Barthes was a theorist who, for biographical and intellectual reasons, always wrote from a position outside of established norms and thus outside of positions of power. A liminal or borderline voice, Barthes's work always questions ideas and positions which are generally agreed upon and are thus powerful, in the sense of being 'common-sensical' and possessing the sanction of state-sponsored institutions. In the most banal of senses this might seem to make Barthes a trouble-maker, a rebel sometimes with, sometimes without a cause; however, Barthes's constantly mutating voice has crucial things to teach us, or remind us, about theory as a discursive practice. Barthes's practice as a writer of theoretical texts constantly changes and mutates; whenever, as a theorist, Barthes senses that an approach, or set of ideas, has become stable, generally accepted, assimilated into a professional, institutional practice, he moves his discourse and his practice somewhere else. He does this because, for him, as for most of the founders of modern theory, the discursive practice of theory must be one which challenges received ideas and questions the orthodoxies which inevitably dominate any language. If one of theory's fundamental purposes is to remind us of the arbitrary, culturally specific nature of all language use, then theory must attack languages which present themselves as stable, universally valid and timeless. Such an attack cannot be carried out if the language theory employs becomes official, orthodox, beyond question. Theory must ensure that its own language resists the processes of assimilation and solidification which it seeks to expose within culture and its institutions: the university, the professionalized world of literature, the modern media.

Barthes was a writer at once ferociously serious as a theorist and yet able to create texts which gained a popular audience. Texts such as *Mythologies*, *A Lover's Discourse* and *Camera Lucida* have a readership which is in no way confined within the limits of academic syllabi and scholarly debate. This should not lead us, however, to confuse Barthes with contemporary academics who 'popularize' academic research for a mass audience on television and in commercial newspapers and journals. Barthes was not a popularist but rather a theorist who was committed to the destruction of commonly held ideas, whether these ideas reside in the specialized realms of academic disciplines or in mass culture itself. Barthes's project as a theorist, then, was to unsettle every idea which took on the appearance of being natural or commonsensical or indisputable. This commitment to critique and questioning is, or at least should be, the characteristic feature of what we call 'theory'. Barthes exemplifies this feature in all his work, but he performs the task in a style of writing which, if often technical, is rarely anything but exquisitely formed. A theorist who directed his attention to all facets of cultural and intellectual life, Barthes's work has an immediacy and a relevance that is rarely attained by other theorists.

THIS BOOK

There are numerous entry points into the work of Roland Barthes. Readers concerned with literature often begin to read him through essays such as 'The Death of the Author' or 'Introduction to the

Structural Analysis of Narratives'. Those concerned with photography usually begin with his essay 'The Rhetoric of the Image' or his last book, *Camera Lucida*. Students doing cultural analysis and cultural studies may well begin with *Mythologies* or essays such as 'The Third Meaning', while those concerned with the history of literature might begin with *Writing Degree Zero* or essays such as 'The Reality Effect'. Despite the great attention that Barthes has always attracted, however, there remain areas of his work which have yet to provoke sufficient response. Barthes's work on theatre and performance has not attracted the attention it deserves. His complex and profoundly theoretical approach to writing as a gay man still offers huge challenges and resources for modern readers and practitioners of 'queer theory'. There are many different 'Barthes' available to readers, then, not least because those readers come to him from many different locations and with various interests and preoccupations.

This book attempts to serve Barthes's different readers by locating a set of key ideas and structuring each chapter around them. It is also important, however, to gain a sense of the different phases through which Barthes passed as a writer, teacher and intellectual. The chapters in this book, therefore, also register a certain chronology, moving from Barthes's early phase in Chapters 1 and 2, through his work on semiology and structuralism in Chapters 3 and 4, onto his post-structuralist phase in Chapters 5 and 6, and finally onto a set of issues emerging from his later writings from Chapters 7 to 9. The benefit of presenting Barthes's key ideas in a relatively chronological order is that readers can begin to see significant relations between ideas they would otherwise experience in isolation. The idea of commitment analysed in Chapter 1, for example, recurs sporadically throughout the rest of the book, as do other key ideas, in particular, Barthes's life-long analysis of the manner in which culture assimilates radical, avant-garde concepts and modes of expression. Other ideas, such as intertextuality or Barthes's concern with hedonist philosophy, occur at specific moments of his writing career, and yet reading Barthes from first to last allows us to contextualize such ideas within the broader, more enduring themes evident within his entire body of work.

Readers of this book, differing as they are in their interests and motivations, may find it useful to break the chronology of the study and begin with, for example, Chapters 3 and 4 and the issue of semiology and structuralism, or Chapters 8 and 9 which deal with with Barthes's work on photography and music. The account of the journey which Barthes went through as a writer and intellectual, however, will be of great use in illuminating and contextualizing specific ideas and issues. Along with the chapters on Barthes's key ideas, this book adds a further chapter, 'After Barthes', which examines the importance and relevance of those ideas today and discusses what it means to talk about Barthes's continuing influence. The sense of the overall shape and trajectory of Barthes's work developed in the main chapters of this book is consolidated and developed by the inclusion of a section on 'Further Reading' which describes briefly each of Barthes's major texts. This section can be used in various ways. Barthes wrote so many books that his oeuvre can at times seem daunting and overwhelming. The 'Further Reading' section helps to provide a simplified map of Barthes's major texts which readers may wish to consult as they read the main chapters of this book. Within this section is included an annotated list of texts on Barthes, aimed to help those readers who wish to pursue further study. This list is not exhaustive, but it does demonstrate the current vitality of work on Barthes's legacy as a writer and thinker, and the diversity of the discussion his work has produced.

KEY IDEAS

KEY IDEAS

1

WRITING AND LITERATURE

This chapter deals with Barthes's first major publication, *Writing Degree Zero* (1953), and that work's engagement with the twin influences of Marxist theory and Existentialist philosophy and literature. Barthes's first book is a sustained engagement with these influences, particularly as they are manifested in the work of Jean-Paul Sartre (1905–80). To understand Barthes's early work, and thus to build a foundation for an understanding of his most important ideas, we need to look at Sartre's major engagement with literary theory and literary history, and then at how Barthes develops and revises it.

COMMITMENT: THE INFLUENCE OF SARTRE

Roland Barthes entered the French critical scene in the 1950s, a period in which tensions and conflicts emanating from the Second World War still dominated French society and culture. One question often features in official histories of this period. As one historian has phrased the question: is post-war French modernization an attempt on the part of French society to wash itself clean of the 'stains' of Nazi occupation? (Ross 1995). That is to say, was France wholly a victim or in some senses a participant (in the form of the Vichy government) in the evil of Fascism? Compounding this ambivalence, and thus perhaps the push towards modernization, the 1950s also saw its colonial past returning to disturb French society, as in the struggle for independence of the African colony of Algeria (full independence from France was granted after eight years of war in April 1962).

The ambiguities just mentioned are accompanied by a developing global conflict. It is in the 1950s that the cold war between the US and the Soviet Union 'hots up'. Radical French intellectuals, writers and thinkers who would contribute to the liberation of social and cultural life, find themselves, in the 1950s, in something of a no man's land. Unable to accept their government's endorsement of American-style capitalism, they are made uneasy by the stifling and rigid character of Soviet-influenced Marxism, symbolized on a political and human level by the Russian invasion of Hungary in 1956.

Nowhere were these tensions and ambiguities more vividly and productively felt than in the work of Jean-Paul Sartre. A philosopher, novelist, playwright and literary critic, Sartre was a towering figure in French intellectual thought from the 1930s until the 1970s. Among his numerous contributions to thought, Sartre was the leading figure of the philosophical and literary movement known as Existentialism.

Sartre's *What is Literature?* (1947) is an attempt, on the basis of Existentialist philosophy, to answer the question posed by his title. Barthes was later to state, in an interview in 1975: 'Sartre brought me into modern literature' (GV: 327). To understand Barthes's early work we have to look at the text which, above all others, provided Barthes with the foundation upon which he began to build his own career. *What is Literature?* posits literature as an exchange between writer and reader. The writer demands that the reader call upon his freedom to read authentically (rather than in some socially preprogrammed manner) and the reader in turn demands that the writer make this demand upon him (Sartre 2001: 41). Authors write, Sartre argues, 'so that free men may feel their freedom as they face it' (Sartre 2001: 47). This model of writing hinges on the notion of *commitment*, the writer's (and the reader's) commitment to address, to call upon, their own and other people's human freedom.

Sartre, however, is fully aware that the Existentialist language of commitment and freedom is, if not utopian, then at least idealistic. Society puts a considerable amount of pressure on individuals to con-form, to practise 'bad faith'. A great deal of *What is Literature?* is concerned with what limits the freedom and the commitment of the writer. Two interrelated approaches are taken to this crucial issue:

EXISTENTIALISM

Existentialism is a complex and now long-established philosophical tradition with many distinct forms and varieties. Despite the many differences which exist between writers associated with the term, Existentialism can be said to focus philosophy on human existence within the world. Rejecting other dominant philosophical concerns with establishing foundations for ethics, or logic, or other universal principles, Existentialism begins with a consideration of human existence and the possibilities open to individual human beings within the world in which they find themselves (see Langiulli 1997: 1–30). In France, Existentialism in philosophy, literature and the arts is particularly associated with the post-war influence of Sartre's writings, an influence which was dominant from the 1940s through to the beginning of the 1970s. Sartre's version of Existentialism takes up the philosophical notion that 'existence precedes essence' in arguing that human beings have the freedom to make themselves into what they are potentially: rational, liberated from false ideas and modes of living. It is 'bad faith' to argue that you have no choice in what you think and how you live your life, that 'essence' precedes 'existence' (Sartre 1956). Post-war Existentialism emerges from sustained terror, from the experience of 'man at his limit' (Solomon 1988: 178–9). How can we argue that human beings are free to create themselves after the Holocaust? How can we argue that human beings have a responsibility to awaken, to activate, their 'freedom to be' after the genocide of Hitler's and other Fascist regimes? Existentialism frequently answers these questions through the concept of 'negation'. Even in the worst circumstances human beings are still free to negate the world around them, to recognize its falseness, its evilness, its absurdity. Existentialist literature, in writers such as Sartre, Albert Camus (1913–60), Simone de Beauvoir (1908–86) and others, often presents individuals confronting an apparently unyielding and unremitting natural or social world only to recognize, in however limited a form, their own freedom of thought and the absurdity of the world which confronts them.

a history of the development of literature (viewed in terms of the changing relationship between writers and readers); a review of the current position of the writer in post-war France. Sartre produces a history of the whole of French literature, but his main focus is on how literature has changed over the preceding two hundred years. Literature has

BOURGEOISIE

Originally a term for someone who dealt (conducted business) in the city. In the work of Karl Marx (1818–83) and Friedrich Engels (1820–95), the bourgeoisie are contrasted with the proletariat. The latter are working men and women who are exploited under capitalism; the former are the owners of capital, that is men (rarely women) who own the means of production (factories, large businesses) and who pay wages. As Simon Blackburn states, such a definition of the word excludes 'the intermediate middle class, whose labour is supervisory and intellectual' (Blackburn 1994: 47). The fact is, however, that the word comes at least in France to take on huge significance and to include the whole gamut of people (capitalist owners, professionals, intellectuals, teachers, business people of all sizes) who can be distinguished from the working class and from what little remaining aristocracy survives. The enlargement of the reference of the word, in fact, goes hand-in-hand with the emergence of modern capitalist (commercial, consumerist, business-oriented) society in France. At times writers, attempting to remember the original Marxist definition of the term, distinguish between the bourgeoisie proper and what they call the petit bourgeoisie. By the latter they mean the equivalent to what in England gets called the 'lower middle class'. Writers such as Sartre and Barthes, however, are not simply referring to a class of people in society when they employ the term bourgeois. They also refer to bourgeois culture, by which they mean the dominant culture (based on the bourgeois values of commercialism and consumerism) of modern-day France. Post-war France, according to Sartre and Barthes, is bourgeois: dominated by the bourgeois class and by the values of that class.

developed in this period, Sartre argues, within the context of the rise to dominance of a social class, the bourgeoisie.

Sartre argues that bourgeois authors writing before the French Revolution (1789) could express commitment by writing for and to the members of their own class. Since the desire for increased power within the bourgeoisie seemed to be the expression of a desire for a more equal society, writing to and for the bourgeoisie could, prior to the Revolution, be squared with notions of commitment. Increasingly, however, in the subsequent century and a half after the Revolution, the bourgeois author has been faced with an audience which becomes increasingly dominant, both politically and culturally. The modern author (and Sartre argues that all notable modern authors are bourgeois) does not want to write for and to his own class, his immediate audience. To do so, in a reversal pivoting around the Revolution, is to write in confirmation of a class which now possesses power and thus the means of social and cultural oppression. The modern author, in this sense, is alienated. Wishing to express his or her commitment to human and social freedom, which invariably means the possibility of an equal and indeed classless society, the modern writer's audience (the bourgeois literate public) is precisely the audience for whom he does not wish to write. On this basis, Sartre produces a history of modern literature in which literature increasingly attacks its audience and adopts strategies of non-communication. Sartre's argument, in fact, is a resounding critique of the idea of the avant-garde in literature.

For Sartre, the forms of avant-garde literature which have arisen in the modern period of French cultural history are an expression of alienation (a hatred or loathing of the author's own culture and audience), rather than expressions of authentic literary commitment. The situation, in fact, can seem very bleak when we examine Sartre's account of the contemporary scene. The author who would be committed cannot use the forms of bourgeois culture itself (popular forms of a purely commercialized culture), nor, it would seem, can he or she employ the techniques of avant-garde literature without falling into a relationship of

AVANT-GARDE

The word 'avant-garde' originally stems from military discourse denoting the 'advanced guard', those in front, in advanced positions, those who go before the main assault (see Cuddon 1991: 74). In relation to literature, and art generally, it comes, in the nineteenth century, to be used to refer to forms of art which are innovative in form, radically challenging in their modes of presentation: these movements include Symbolism, Surrealism, Dadaism, and, in the post-Second World War period, the nouveau roman (the 'new novel', see Chapter 2, pp. 28–31). A common critical assumption relates avant-garde forms of art with politically radical agendas and motives. It can be argued, however, that simply because a work of art is radical in its form this does not necessarily make it radical in its political intentions or influence.

non-communication with the general public. Avant-garde art, according to Sartre, cannot be committed, since it does not wish to communicate directly. The apparent lack of choice for the modern author is exacerbated by the cold war political climate. Unable to accept Western capitalism, Sartre is doubtful about Soviet Communism and its representative in France (the PCF: Parti communiste français, the French Communist Party). Despite the influence of Marxism on his thought, Sartre in *What is Literature?* sees the PCF as deeply suspicious of intellectuals and all writers save those who acquiesce to its rigid ideological prescriptions. The modern writer, it would seem, has no viable form for writing, and no viable political allegiance: 'we have fallen outside history and are speaking in the desert', Sartre writes (2001: 205).

Despite its historical and contemporary diagnosis of the condition and position of the writer, *What is Literature?* ends with a reaffirmation of Sartrean Existentialism. Even in such an apparently bleak situation, Sartre argues, we can still practise our commitment to a better world; authors can still challenge themselves and their readers to be free. 'Man', Sartre defiantly writes, 'must be invented each day' (2001: 226).

We need to attend to Sartre's arguments in *What is Literature?* since they form the context for Barthes's most important early work, *Writing Degree Zero*. While Barthes's book mirrors many of the themes and preoccupations to be found in Sartre's study, it disagrees fundamentally about the idea of commitment. The key to this comes when we register the fact that, despite Sartre's optimism, there is no real sense in his text of what kind of writing would, in fact, constitute a committed kind. There is a lack of attention to the issue of form in Sartre's analysis, and it is, characteristically, in terms of form – the kind of writing which authors produce – that Barthes conducts his revision and critique of Sartre's arguments.

WRITING, LITERATURE, STYLE

Barthes's *Writing Degree Zero* is divided into two interrelated parts: one theoretical, one historical. The second part provides an alternative history of French literature to the one provided by Sartre. This historical account, however, is presented on the basis of a theoretical analysis of the relationship between language, style and what Barthes calls *écriture* (writing).

Barthes's purpose in refocusing critical attention on language, style and writing is to redefine the contexts within which we can understand the idea of commitment. If commitment concerns the choices an author makes, as we have seen Sartre arguing, then, according to Barthes, we must attend to the confines within which authors exercise their freedom to choose. Authors exist and make their choices within language. More importantly, they exist within literary language which has pre-existing forms, conventions, genres and codes. No author simply invents his or her own literary language. All authors create their works out of a struggle with the already established language of literature.

Barthes's argument begins by distinguishing language and style from writing. Language and style are not areas of choice. The language of a given nation at a given time, such as the French language in the 1850s or the 1950s, is not something any author can make decisions about: it exists as a kind of 'Nature' for the author, a 'resistant medium' (WDZ: 11–12). Language, in this sense, is the medium presented to the author, the sea within which he or she must learn to swim. Style is something else, however. Barthes argues that style comes involuntarily from the author's body. Style, that is to say, derives from the author's personal history and the nature of his or her personality. Once again, style, like language, is not something that the author can choose (WDZ: 14). Against language and style, conceived in this fashion, Barthes introduces a third idea, writing.

Writing has a major part to play in Barthes's entire career, and indeed in the emergence of structuralist and particularly post-structuralist thought within the French intellectual scene of the 1960s. Barthes comments on the significant role the idea of writing plays in his and other theorists' work in a 1971 interview in the journal *Tel Quel*, but he also notes the different meanings given to the word between the early 1950s and the early 1970s (Res: 263–4). We will return to the idea of writing on a number of occasions in this study.

In *Writing Degree Zero*, writing is used to represent that aspect of the author's activity which can involve choice and thus commitment. Writing, here, concerns what we might call *form*, a set of codes and conventions which the author shares with a specific community. The opening paragraph of the book presents the reader with a vivid example of writing in this sense:

> Hébert, the revolutionary, never began a number of his news-sheet *Le Père Duchêne* without introducing a sprinkling of obscenities. These improprieties had no real meaning, but they had significance. In what way? In that they expressed a whole revolutionary situation. Now here is an example of a mode of writing whose function is no longer only communication or expression, but the imposition of something beyond language, which is both History and the stand we take in it.
>
> (WDZ: 3)

Sartre had seen the issue of commitment within a strictly communicational model. Committed writing, for Sartre, must convey a message, an image of the world and a sense of what it is and might be to be human. For Sartre it makes no sense to talk about a committed form of literature without discussing the message which literature communicates to its audience. Indeed, for Sartre, a defining sign of the lack of commitment in a good deal of modern literature is found precisely in its refusal to communicate to its audience in this fashion. Barthes disagrees with Sartre's position and argues that writing is, in its extreme forms, an 'anticommunication' (WDZ: 19).

Barthes's notion of writing concerns that which is communicated outside or beyond any message or content. The writing of Jacques Hébert (1757–94), with its aggressive and defiant expletives, conveys a commitment to revolutionary politics in its form, not in the ideas conveyed through that form. There is meaning in this kind of writing which has nothing to do with the ideas being conveyed and everything to do with the way those ideas are being conveyed. Hébert's characteristic opening expletives are, we should note, not a question of style. If they were part of Hébert's style, they would merely signify something unique about him as an individual writer. Hébert, in that case, would merely be an author whose style involved excessive cursing. On the contrary, Hébert's opening expletives signify something beyond himself, they link him to an available (revolutionary) attitude towards society, towards history, towards language itself.

Barthes's idea of writing begins to open up the possibility of a greater link between Sartre's Existentialist account of literature and a Marxist account which would stress the ideological functions of writing in history (Res: 252). That is to say, once we begin to understand writing as the expression of an ideological commitment on the part of the author, we are in a position to begin to study how authors throughout history have responded to social and political realities by choosing distinct forms of expression. This would be a mode of literary history that could read what Barthes calls the 'signs of literature', the way, that is, in which the forms of literature convey social and ideological meanings and choices. In our present period, for example, we might imagine a novelist who chooses to write a realistic novel and a novelist who chooses to write an experimental novel – say, a narrative in a first-person singular voice with no punctuation or paragraphs. These authors are making extremely important choices on the level of form, of writing, which will radically affect the meaning of their work. It may well be that both novelists wish to convey a revolutionary message. Both novelists may wish to communicate the need for a radical change in the ruling social order. Both may believe that such a change can only occur through the liberation of women. Both novelists may be feminists with almost identical social and political beliefs. Their choice of form, of writing, however, will radically affect the meaning of their works. We do not read such different forms of novel in the same way; they are associated with a host of different positions and perspectives which will inevitably affect the manner in which they are received and thus the meaning they generate.

Our hypothetical example, however, raises a serious issue with regard to choice and thus commitment. It is certainly true that authors can choose widely divergent modes of writing, yet they do not invent those modes of writing. For writing to be socially significant, and thus involved in social and political commitment, it must already be existent prior to its adoption by an author. Hébert's expletives would not convey the meaning they do unless people already associated that kind of language in that particular situation (the beginning of an editorial piece in a political publication) as revolutionary.

Having linked commitment to writing, Barthes is quick to point out that writing is still confined, that it does not offer up the possibility of an unlimited freedom: 'It is not granted to the writer to choose his mode of writing from a kind of non-temporal store of literary forms. It is under the pressure of History and Tradition that the possible modes of writing for a given writer are established; there is a History of Writing' (WDZ: 16). This point is crucial for Barthes's whole argument in *Writing Degree Zero* and it is one of the features which links this book to his subsequent structuralist and post-structuralist work.

Barthes describes any mode of writing available to the author as vacillating between 'freedom and remembrance' (WDZ: 17). As we have seen, it is in choosing forms of writing that an author's freedom lies; and yet all forms of writing possess within them an 'after-image', traces of their prior use. We might think of the example of Hébert again. The expletives Hébert uses are said, by Barthes, to communicate a commitment to revolutionary political action. Yet, at some point, if a writer continues in such a vein, the significance of such a mode of writing will change and become merely *what that kind of writer does* or even a completely expected aspect of writing amounting to a universally recognized code or convention. Writing, that is to say, striving to embody a choice and a commitment in the author, is constantly in danger of becoming merely a kind of cliché, something which pigeonholes the author. Barthes refers to this process as 'a progressive solidification' (WDZ: 6) and as a 'dramatic phenomenon of concretion' (WDZ: 5). Writing, Barthes argues, is constantly solidifying into Literature (in this regard it is best to follow Barthes's practice and use the upper case), into what Barthes at one point calls by the very traditional name 'Belles-Lettres' (WDZ: 33). To understand why Literature should be so negatively figured in the argument of *Writing Degree Zero* we have to move to the parallel dimension of Barthes's argument in the book, his argument concerning modern literary history.

ZERO-DEGREE WRITING

Barthes's account of literary history, as we have already noted, takes off from the account presented in Sartre's *What is Literature?* Like Sartre, Barthes bases his history on the emergence, dominance and then collapse of the bourgeois writer's relationship to bourgeois society and culture. Like Sartre, Barthes presents a history with a pivotal point and thus a 'before' and an 'after' pattern. Barthes shifts Sartre's pivotal moment of 1789 forwards to 1848, a year of renewed revolution in France and across Europe. However, in a similar manner to Sartre, he describes the period before his transitional date as one in which the bourgeois writer identifies with his society and thus his audience. After 1848, with the consolidation of bourgeois cultural and social dominance, the writer begins to feel increasingly alienated from his or her surroundings, no longer possessing that supreme confidence that his or her language and consciousness is shared by the rest of society.

So far, this seems to replicate Sartre's historical thesis. However, Barthes's approach stresses that literature is no innocent party in this situation of alienation and search for freedom. Literature, like everything else in modern society, is owned by the bourgeoisie. Literature is an institution and a site of power which absorbs into itself and reworks for its own purposes all cultural practices.

Barthes's arguments here are close to those made by a group of German Marxist theorists and intellectuals from the 1920s onwards, collectively known as the Frankfurt School. One of that movement's leading thinkers, Theodor Adorno (1903–69), refers to what he calls the modern 'culture industry', by which he means the manner in which contemporary capitalist society accommodates all artistic practices into its own processes of commercialism and commodification. A quick look at our current society in which, with staggering speed, the latest radical form of music or new mode of political action is represented back to us in terms of advertising campaigns, media discussion and the content and style of commercial cinema or television, should explain the pertinence of such a diagnosis of modern culture. Similarly, for Barthes in *Writing Degree Zero*, modern Literature absorbs all forms of writing into itself, like some kind of irresistible vacuum cleaner.

Barthes explains and expands upon this view of Literature by enumerating a succession of strategies by which authors since the 1850s have struggled to resist absorption into Literature, into bourgeois 'Letters'. His first example is focused on Gustave Flaubert (1821–80), an author practising his art at precisely the pivotal moment of the 1840s and 1850s. Barthes refers to what he calls the 'Flaubertization' of writing, by which he means a move to a notion of writing as 'hard work', a laborious craft. Writers such as Flaubert, in other words, attempted to cure their increasing sense of alienation from bourgeois Literature by figuring themselves as workers, craftsmen and craftswomen. It is obvious, however, how easily such a strategy can be absorbed by dominant culture and transformed into bourgeois cultural values which have always in themselves emphasized hard work and perseverance.

Barthes's pessimistic diagnosis of the situation of the modern writer begins to be registered here and seems connected less to Sartre's austere optimism that we can always choose to be free than to Camus's sense of the absurdity of modern existence. In his *The Myth of Sisyphus*, for example, Camus compares modern men and women struggling for freedom with the legendary King Sisyphus who was condemned, in the underworld, to roll forever a rock up to the top of a steep hill, only for it to roll back down again. Likewise, the Flaubertian strategy of hard work, meant to cure the modern author of the alienation of bourgeois Literature, merely deepens his or her writing's relation to the ethics and values of bourgeois Literature. The modern writer, for Barthes, is a Sisyphean figure, continually striving to create a free writing, continually experiencing the collapse of that writing into Literature. Barthes's thesis is pessimistic, but it is also more thoroughly Marxist than Sartre's in its sense of the relation between writing and society. If the historical situation of human society is alienated, then writing cannot but participate in that alienation.

An even more important and far-reaching example follows the discussion of Flaubert's strategy of hard work, that being the emergence in the nineteenth century of the realist novel. Realism and Naturalism (nowadays a less commonly used term) set out to cure the alienation of literary writing by producing an accurate and artless form. One definition of realism in the novel which is still employed in university courses today is as follows: '*Realism*, a form of writing which does not bring attention to its own artifice, its own constructedness'. Barthes's thesis is, however, confirmed in that very definition, since the realist novel, so dominant from the mid-nineteenth century to the present, is by definition an alienated form of writing, hiding its literariness at the same time as establishing this mode as *the* standard of 'good writing', of 'literary' writing. Barthes refers to the fact that the realist novel is at one and the same time the kind of novel still privileged in bourgeois schools and the kind of novel officially sanctioned by Soviet Communism and its international off-shoots, such as the PCF (WDZ: 58–61). The realist novel, far from creating an unalienated mode of writing, has become the 'sign of Literature' for both bourgeois and anti-bourgeois culture. Its conventions – the use of the third person ('he', 'they') or the use of the first-person voice of a character ('I'), certain characteristic tenses and adjectives, a particularly detailed attention to objects – all go to build up what Barthes, in subsequent contributions to this critique of realism, will call 'the reality effect' (see 'The Reality Effect', RL: 141–8). Thus, a mode of writing that was created initially in an attempt to move beyond literary conventions towards an accurate representation of the social world, ends by establishing tenacious codes and conventions for the creation of the illusion of reality.

Strategies devised to cure Literature, Barthes goes on to argue, are replaced in the latter part of the nineteenth century by strategies of a far more aggressive nature. If Literature cannot be cured, then it seems it must be killed, assassinated, completely negated, 'dislocated'. Writing, for many modern writers, becomes an attempt to murder Literature. Barthes here is referring to the tendency in Modernist modes of writing, such as those found in the poetry of Stephane Mallarmé (1842–98) and those who followed him, to eradicate within their writing all signs of Literature. This is a writing which seeks to strip its language of all convention, to free itself from all recognizable narrative and poetic codes. This, however, Barthes argues, is a revolutionary writing that can only lead to silence, to a 'complete abandonment of communication' (RL: 63). This tendency relates to another strategy, which is the one which gives Barthes's book its title. Barthes refers to authors who attempt to produce a 'colourless writing, freed from all bondage to a pre-ordained state of language'. 'The aim here', he goes on, 'is to go beyond Literature by entrusting one's fate to a sort of basic speech, equally far from living languages and from literary language proper' (RL: 64). This writing, which achieves an almost 'ideal absence of style', is exemplified for Barthes by Camus's novel *L'Étranger* (*The Outsider/The Stranger*), originally published in 1942. Taking a term from linguistics, Barthes describes this kind of writing as 'neutral', 'inert' or the 'degree zero' of writing and states that it 'remains wholly responsible, without being overlaid by a secondary commitment of form to a History not its own' (RL: 64). In other words, this kind of zero-degree writing avoids the contamination of Literature. Camus's novel famously begins:

> Mother died today. Or maybe yesterday, I don't know. I had a telegram from the home: 'Mother passed away. Funeral tomorrow. Yours sincerely.' That doesn't mean anything. It may have been yesterday.
>
> (Camus 2000: 9)

In an 'Afterword', first published in 1955, Camus described his character Meursault as someone who is an outsider to society because he is someone who refuses to lie. Camus goes on to define what he means by lying: 'Lying is not only saying what isn't true. It is also, in fact especially, saying more than is true and, in the case of the human heart, saying more than one feels' (Camus 2000: 118). This is an excellent definition of what Barthes sees in Camus's writing, given that for Barthes 'lying' can be substituted by the word Literature. If Literature is that which adds unwanted meanings, conventional associations, the codes of tradition and dominant ideology to writing, then Camus's neutral, 'colourless' writing seems to avoid such trappings, such additional meanings. Camus's degree-zero writing refuses to lie, appears 'honest' (WDZ: 65).

By the time Barthes has reached his description of degree-zero writing in Camus, however, he has elaborated a thesis, both theoretical and historical, which cannot allow for such a writing to succeed for more than a moment. If writing cannot be free while society (and history) are 'in chains', then the very processes of absorption and assimilation into Literature and thus dominant culture will inevitably occur with regard to this mode of writing as well. Barthes writes:

> Unfortunately, nothing is more fickle than a colourless writing; mechanical habits are developed in the very place where freedom existed, a network of set forms hem in more and more the pristine freshness of discourse. . . . The writer, taking his place as a 'classic,' becomes the slavish imitator of his original creation, society demotes his writing to a mere manner, and returns him a prisoner to his own formal myths.
>
> (WDZ: 65)

It is certainly true that many schoolchildren outside of France are nowadays presented with *L'Étranger* as *the* classic example of 'clear' and, by implication, 'good' French literature. Bourgeois culture has assimilated (acculturated) Camus's writing as surely as it has assimilated the nineteenth-century realist novel.

Barthes's ultimate point, therefore, seems to be pessimistic. If society is alienated then so, necessarily, is literary writing. The modern writer is a 'tragic' figure: 'However hard he tries to create a free language, it comes back to him fabricated. . . . Writing therefore is a blind alley, and it is because society itself is a blind alley' (WDZ: 72). Instead of calling such a thesis pessimistic, however, it would be more accurate to call it 'dialectical'.

Barthes's account of writing is dialectical in that it understands freedom within the context of a conflict with convention and tradition.

Writers cannot, in the modern world, simply choose to be free, to eradicate from their language all traces of a stifling tradition. They cannot, however, cease the pursuit of a free language without ceasing to be writers in any meaningful sense. As Barthes puts the case:

> literary writing carries at the same time the alienation of History and the dream of History; as a Necessity, it testifies to the division of languages which is inseparable from the division of classes; as Freedom, it is the consciousness of this division and the very effort which seeks to surmount it.
>
> (WDZ: 73)

This dialectical account of modern writing is crucial at the commencement of Barthes's career, since it can be said, paradoxically, to empower him as a critic. An effective analysis of the place of *Writing Degree Zero* in Barthes's career, as the next chapter will demonstrate, must eventually focus on the consequences the thesis articulated in that book has not only for modern literary writers but also for Barthes himself, as a critical writer.

SUMMARY

In this chapter we have seen how Barthes responds to Sartre's idea of commitment in literature by refocusing critical attention on form, particularly writing as it is defined in *Writing Degree Zero*. Unlike Sartre, Barthes views literary form itself as an ideological medium and thus something which can communicate social commitment. However, Barthes remains intensely conscious of the manner in which new, radically innovative forms are quickly absorbed by bourgeois culture. Barthes's argument in *Writing Degree Zero* eventuates, therefore, in a position which will reverberate throughout his later work: the committed contemporary writer, for Barthes, is someone who strives for an authentic writing while knowing that all forms, all modes of writing, will eventually be assimilated by and into Literature.

2

CRITICAL DISTANCE

This chapter continues our examination of Barthes's early work by looking at the manner in which he developed the argument outlined in *Writing Degree Zero*. In a series of essays written and published in the late 1950s and early 1960s, Barthes applied the ideas presented in his first book to the realms of contemporary fiction and drama. Within the context of this continuation of the argument of *Writing Degree Zero* it is also necessary to consider Barthes's second book, his study of the nineteenth-century French historian Michelet. By beginning with *Michelet*, it is possible, in fact, to establish a general emphasis in Barthes's early work on the need for critical and historical distance.

MICHELET

Barthes's thesis in *Writing Degree Zero* means that, as a critic, it makes no sense for him to simply champion one particular mode of writing, one particular literary movement. Support for the most radical modes of writing might seem an obvious move for an avowedly Marxist critic outside of the influence of official Communist party allegiances. However, such a critical move would run against the grain of Barthes's position, since, as he demonstrated in his first book, every temporarily committed and free mode of writing eventually collapses back into convention and Literature. On the basis of Barthes's argument in *Writing*

Degree Zero, the commitment of the critic must be not to one mode of writing, one literary or intellectual movement, but must rather be a kind of free-floating and constantly adaptable engagement with all available modes and movements of writing. Since 'freedom', as it is expressed in *Writing Degree Zero*, concerns the temporary moment of authentic writing, the flash of meaning and form as yet unassimilated by normative culture, freedom and commitment for the critic must involve the ability to pursue every kind of literary writing, classical or modern, avant-garde or mainstream. In the 1971 *Tel Quel* interview cited in the last chapter (p. 15), Barthes figures the position he has adopted as a critic in very personal terms (involving a love of certain forms of writing), but his main point is to affirm his position between cultural and historical trends: 'my own historical position . . . is to be at the *rear-guard of the avant-garde*: to be avant-garde one must know what is dead; to be rear-guard, one must still love it . . . this is, I think, the exact place of what I write' (Res: 263).

Barthes's work as a critic in the decade subsequent to the publication of *Writing Degree Zero* (we shall deal with *Mythologies*, first published in 1957, in the next chapter) was to spread itself, if not equally then certainly conspicuously, over classical, bourgeois and avant-garde subjects. Barthes's *Michelet*, for example, a book he had researched over a long period stretching back to his sanitorium days, deals with a historian who seems to have precisely the opposite motivation for writing to the one endorsed in *Writing Degree Zero*. As Barthes puts it: 'politically, Michelet had no original views, he had only the average ideas of the petite-bourgeoisie around 1840' (M: 203).

To take as a subject a nineteenth-century historian of such a petit-bourgeois character might seem a strange decision after *Writing Degree Zero*. Yet, as Barthes explains, we should not read Michelet (1798–1874) for what he tells us about history; he tells us very little. We should read Michelet as a writer. While history itself changes, and indeed while Michelet's own views change throughout his long and prodigiously productive life, Michelet's writing (on the level of form and style) remains constant. Barthes is concerned to show, in fact, the manner in which Michelet absorbs history (historical facts, the normative data of historical discourse) into the on-going 'themes' of his writing. Barthes states: 'the theme sustains a whole system of values; no theme is neutral, and all the substance of the world is divided up into beneficent and maleficent states' (ibid.). The themes, as described by Barthes in the bulk of the study, are extremely idiosyncratic. Michelet works, on this level, through a language of the body, dividing whole epochs, historical movements and events into sensual categories of warmth, dryness, fecundity, emptiness and so on. Hence, as Barthes demonstrates, for Michelet the Jesuits are negatively dry, while Germany is positively warm. A whole symbolic logic is unveiled through the critical elucidation of these categories. The Jesuits, being dry, for example, are connected to industrialization and other forms of modernization disapproved of by Michelet. Germany, on the other hand, is connected to positive terms such as 'the People' and female menstruation, the latter being a peculiarly positive phenomenon for Michelet as a man and a writer.

In a later essay on Michelet first published in the journal *L'Arc* in 1972, Barthes takes up the argument of his earlier study and declares that it is useless to judge Michelet as a historian in terms of modern criteria (RL: 199–200). We need, rather, to recognize and foreground the *distance* between his writing and our current views concerning history and indeed writing itself. Barthes's *Michelet* can be understood, then, as an original contribution to the study of historical discourse, in that it gives back to one of France's most important but increasingly neglected historians his strangeness, his distance.

Barthes's point goes further than simply honouring the distance of a writer such as Michelet, however. It is, he argues, only by recognizing the distance of such a writer that we also begin to be able to judge the relevance of Michelet for modern historical theory and practice. Michelet's relevance, in fact, is huge, since it is with him that we begin to see a questioning of the objectivity of historical writing. This critique of history's claim to be objective has been a major feature of structuralist, post-structuralist and other recent theoretical movements, such as the new historicism. Barthes's treatment of Michelet, not as a historian but as a writer, presents an early contribution to that modern intellectual trend and provides us, in Michelet, with a nineteenth-century historian who exemplifies many recent points about history's 'literary qualities'. By registering the strangeness (the distance) of Michelet's work, Barthes is able, eventually, to highlight a very contemporary feature within that work, namely its basis in what we have seen Barthes calling 'language, style and writing'.

The distancing process found in *Michelet* also occurs in Barthes's much debated monograph on the classic French playwright Jean Racine (1639–99). Racinian tragic drama is the classic mode of dramatic writing in orthodox and academic French literary tradition. Functioning rather as Shakespearean drama does in English literary history, Racinian tragic drama *is* tradition within French Literature. Barthes's *On Racine*, a collection of three essays merging Marxist, psychoanalytical and other contemporary critical theories, ultimately seeks to distance Racinian drama in a manner analogous to the distancing of Micheletist history. Barthes attacks the bourgeois critical reading of Racine and particularly its argument that there is something universal within Racine's writing. This assessment of the universal relevance and significance of Racine is a myth, an attempt on the part of bourgeois culture to claim that its own values and desires are mirrored in France's greatest playwright. Barthes writes:

> the myth of Racine is essentially a security operation: it seeks to domesticate Racine, to strip him of his tragic elements, to identify him with ourselves, to locate ourselves with him in the noble salon of classic art ... it seeks to give the themes of the bourgeois theatre an eternal status.
>
> (OR: 149)

Racinian theatre, however, does not speak directly to our own contemporary world and it cannot be transformed into the values of modern, bourgeois theatre (psychology, realism, the struggle of the individual against and within social reality) without losing sight of its strangeness and distance. It is only by attempting to capture and represent that strangeness and distance, Barthes argues, that we can begin to learn again from Racine, rather than simply using his theatre as a myth to defend modern values: 'If we want to keep Racine, we must keep him at a distance' (ibid.).

THE AVANT-GARDE: THE 'NOUVEAU ROMAN' AND BRECHTIAN THEATRE

The emphasis on distance and strangeness that we find in Barthes's work of this period (1953–63) helps us to link his work on bourgeois and classic literature to his concern with more radical and avant-garde literary trends: notably, the politically radical theatre of Bertolt Brecht (1898–1956) and the emergence of the 'nouveau roman' (the 'new novel'), particularly with regard to the novels of Alain Robbe-Grillet

(1922–). Barthes attended the Berliner Ensemble's performance of Brecht's *Mother Courage* at the Paris international festival in May 1954 (see Calvet 1994: 111) and his response was extremely positive, seeing within Brecht's approach a properly Marxist theatre which successfully avoided the pitfalls of bourgeois theatre. The essence of Brecht's theatre lies in its resistance to 'psychology'. It refuses, in other words, to allow for an easy identification of audience with dramatic characters. Brecht's famous 'Distancing Effect' (sometimes referred to as the 'Alienation Effect') generated a style of performance in which the audience is never allowed to forget that they are watching a play, a representation of reality rather than reality itself. In this sense, Brecht's theatre produces a distancing effect between audience and actors which is analogous to the distancing between reader and text which Barthes seeks to produce in his works on Michelet and Racine. The purpose of Brechtian distancing, or alienation, is also relatable to Barthes's work on Michelet and Racine in that it seeks to produce an active, critical engagement in the audience (CE: 34–5).

In Brecht's play the audience witnesses Mother Courage's struggles during the Thirty Years' War. Instead of simply sympathizing with her loss of children and the difficulties of eking out an existence during such troubled times, however, the audience is encouraged to recognize Mother Courage's own blindness; she is 'blind' in her own acceptance of and participation in the war (CE: 34). Simply to identify and sympathize with Mother Courage would be to participate in her own blindness: Mother Courage accepts the war as inevitable, as Natural. She is blind to the fact that things, including herself, could be different. By distancing (alienating) the audience from his character, Brecht encourages the audience to do more than identify or sympathize; he encourages his audience to judge critically and thus to recognize its own potentially creative role in the making of history.

Brechtian theatre is radical, therefore, since, unlike bourgeois theatre, it does not allow us to confuse the theatrical world with the actual world. It distances the one from the other. In so doing, Brechtian theatre makes us question things which society would have us believe are inevitable, Natural. In a similar fashion, Barthes's championing of Alain Robbe-Grillet, exponent of the 'nouveau roman', rests on Robbe-Grillet's radical distancing of his novels from the traditional techniques and values of the bourgeois novel. In a series of articles, republished in *Critical Essays* in 1964, Barthes explored the resistance in Robbe-Grillet's works to the standard novelistic features of story, narrative point of view, metaphor, the symbolic nature of described objects. Robbe-Grillet's novels famously deny his readers the ability to translate the objects meticulously described in them into general symbolic and metaphorical themes. In *Jealousy* (first published in 1957), for example, a narrative voice which is never named and acts merely as a kind of neutral observer, presents a world in which the actions of the few represented characters seem no more significant than the descriptions given of the house (a tropical banana plantation) within which the novel is set, including a series of painstaking descriptions of the remains of squashed centipedes. The effect is to present a novel which is unreadable except on a visual ('optical') level: Robbe-Grillet's novels resist being translated (being 'read') into the established terms of bourgeois Literature and offer us, instead, a pure negativity, the meaninglessness of the world of objects. Human beings, in Robbe-Grillet's novels, are refused the comfort of finding a meaning for their own lives in the objects (natural and man-made) around them. As Barthes puts it: 'Robbe-Grillet describes objects in order to expel man from them' (CE: 94).

Barthes's readings of Robbe-Grillet are clearly an extension of the argument presented in *Writing Degree Zero*. Robbe-Grillet's novels of the pure, meaningless object represent a new attempt to create a kind of novelistic writing free from the confines of bourgeois Literature. However, true to the argument of his first book, Barthes also recognizes that Robbe-Grillet ultimately fails to produce, for anything more than a moment, a purely 'objective literature' (a literature of pure objects). Barthes writes: 'there is no zero degree of form, negativity always turns into positivity' (CE: 92). In his essay 'There Is No Robbe-Grillet School' Barthes argues, despite the positive essays he has written on Robbe-Grillet and other novelists connected to the 'nouveau roman', that this kind of writing is already being assimilated by bourgeois culture through the very labelling of it as an avant-garde movement: 'It is an old trick', Barthes writes, 'of our criticism to proclaim its breadth of views, its modernism, by baptizing *avant-garde* what it can assimilate, thereby economically combining the security of tradition with the *frisson* of novelty' (CE: 95). In an essay of 1956, 'Whose Theatre? Whose *Avant-Garde*?', Barthes also implies that such an unavoidable assimilation relates to radical theatre: 'once the cutting edge of the new language is blunted, the bourgeoisie raises no objection to accommodating it, to appropriating it for its own purposes' (CE: 68).

Barthes's early work can seem pessimistic if we read such essays in isolation. We have seen, however, that, understood in relation to the argument first set out in *Writing Degree Zero*, Barthes's accounts of radical, bourgeois and classic writing are dialectical. In a number of essays of the period he attempts to spell this out by classifying radical writing as that which asks questions without answering them (see CE: 150–61 and 197–204). Writing is radical for Barthes when it interrogates the world, rather than when it gives us answers which appear to explain and justify it. Art is radical, for Barthes, when through its questions it exposes, as in the theatre of Brecht, the meanings bourgeois culture would have us accept as true and natural. This practice of questioning the world makes radical writing a form of criticism. As Barthes writes: 'in a still-alienated society, art must be critical, it must cut off all illusions, even that of "Nature"' (CE: 75). Such statements about literary writing, however, inevitably influence Barthes's sense of the role of critical writing itself, which must, in its turn, as we shall see in the next chapter, radically question literary, but also social and cultural, illusions.

SUMMARY

In this chapter we have looked at Barthes's book *Michelet*, relating it to Barthes's work on the French playwright Racine, but also to Barthes's early critical work on the 'nouveau roman' and modern theatre (bourgeois and Brechtian). The link between these elements, as we have seen, concerns an extension of the argument of *Writing Degree Zero*. For Barthes, in a society dominated by bourgeois values, committed writing must free itself from the conventions of bourgeois culture, including the dominant conventions of realism in the novel and psychology (identification) in drama. Bourgeois culture, however, is tenacious in its assimilation of avant-garde forms. Barthes's response to this apparent impasse is to focus his attention on the attempt to create a distance between writing and what modern society and culture wants us to believe are universal, timeless and thus natural meanings. This distancing can take the form of various contemporary modes of writing, but it is also a responsibility for criticism itself and can be pursued in the critical examination of classical and bourgeois forms, as well as explicitly radical, avant-garde forms.

3

SEMIOLOGY

The next two chapters deal with Barthes's major work in the fields of semiology and structuralism respectively. While the ideas promoted by these theoretical movements influenced Barthes's work until his death in 1980, it is possible to locate a period in which they dominated his writing. This period takes us from the late 1950s, in which Barthes composed his *Mythologies*, to the latter part of the 1960s. Although the two terms, semiology and structuralism, are intimately related, it is possible to distinguish between work primarily concerned with semiology (dealt with in this chapter) and work of a more fundamentally structuralist nature (dealt with in the next chapter).

READING BOURGEOIS CULTURE

Mythologies is one of Barthes's most influential and widely read books. Composed of articles written monthly for the journal *Les Lettres nouvelles* between 1954 and 1956, it was published as a single text in 1957. The English version of the text is available in two smaller collections (see 'Further Reading', p. 142). Barthes's articles were all published under the heading of 'Mythology of the Month' and they range prolifically through a host of subjects. From the tacit conventions of amateur wrestling to the language of advertising, from the descriptions in travel guides through to the French love of wine, from the

MYTH

In ancient Greece myth (*mūthos*) came to mean a fiction. Nowadays usually associated with fictions which include the gods or supernatural forces, myth also has the general meaning of the major fictional stories that have abided since ancient times. Thus myth, while denoting what is fictional, also tends to refer to stories that have an apparently timeless and universal appeal and truth. Barthes's use of the word myth is therefore particularly telling in that what he designates by the term presents itself as natural and even timeless but is, in fact, an expression of a historically specific ideological vision of the world.

media image of Einstein's brain, the visit to Paris of the American evangelist Billy Graham and the ritual of the Tour de France to the image of the newly released Citröen D.S., Barthes's monthly mythologies present a compelling and invariably witty description of French cultural life in the 1950s.

In his 1957 'Preface', Barthes makes clear the connection the project has to his earlier work. If *Writing Degree Zero* and the essays associated with it sought to establish the manner in which bourgeois culture assimilates writing into what Barthes calls Literature, then his reading of the diverse aspects of modern French culture equally demonstrates the tenaciousness of such an assimilative process. Barthes writes:

> The starting point of these reflections was usually a feeling of impatience at the sight of the 'naturalness' with which newspaper, art and commonsense constantly dress up a reality which, even though it is the one we live in, is undoubtedly determined by history.

(MY: 11)

Just as bourgeois Literature assimilates writing into its apparently timeless values, so culture generally, Barthes argues, constantly presents artificial, manufactured and, above all, ideological objects and values as if they were indisputable, unquestionable and natural. Indeed, this process (presenting cultural phenomena as if they were natural) is, for many theorists, what we mean by the word ideology. Ideology, at least in this sense, is the process whereby what is historical and created by specific cultures is presented as if it were timeless, universal and thus natural. At times this process can simply seem the product of a kind of laziness. In 'The Romans in Films' (MY: 26–8), a contemporary movie, *Julius Caesar*, employs an 'insistent' fringe in the hairstyles of its actors in order to generate the illusion of 'Romanness'. In this film, as in so many others, characters who sweat must be anxious. The descriptions of Spain in the popular travel guide, *The Blue Guide*, reduce everything (towns, landscape and inhabitants) to stereotypes and display what Barthes calls 'the disease of thinking in essences' (MY: 75). In 'Bichon and the Blacks' (ET: 35–8), the magazine *Paris-Match* indulges in an infantile narrative of heroic Westerners travelling into 'Cannibal country' while wars in the Far East devastatingly contextualize such simplistic forms of imperialism.

Other examples of ideology (or the naturalization of culturally specific phenomena) are more directly the product of bourgeois disingenuousness. Politicians include photographs of themselves in their electoral prospectuses in order to make themselves seem one of the people and thus outside of ideology. Billy Graham utilizes a series of primitive tricks in order to whip up a mass hysteria and receptivity to his religious and, Barthes adds, stunningly 'stupid' rhetoric. In 'Dominici, or The Triumph of Literature' (MY: 43–6), the legal process which deals with the case of a farmer from the Alps refuses to countenance any form of language other than its own, transforming a specific bourgeois language of psychological values culled largely from novels into the supposedly universal language of all French men and women. Gaston Dominici, with his rural discourse, is legally silenced in this process. In 'Poujade and the Intellectuals' (ET: 127–35), the extreme right-wing politician Pierre Poujade capitalizes on bourgeois stereotypes about intellectuals (unrooted, abstract, ultimately both dreamy and inhuman) to sell his ideology to the petit bourgeoisie.

In between simple-mindedness and maliciousness, however, come the vast majority of the myths studied by Barthes. These are, perhaps, the most interesting examples and the most significant in that they tell us more about the process that Barthes here calls myth. Some of the best examples of these more subtle forms of myth come from the world of advertising. In 'Soap-Powders and Detergents' (MY: 36–8), for example, Barthes begins to analyse the manner in which certain substances are given specific ideological meanings within culture. Despite the fact that both Persil (a soap-powder) and Omo (a detergent) are made by the one firm, Unilever, a whole categorization of substances rules their presentation. Soap-powders like Persil are presented as creamy, separating agents which liberate clothes from stains, while detergents like Omo, based on chlorine and ammonia, are seen in terms of fire and thus perform a kind of purging and penetration which wages a war on dirt. Persil polices stains, while Omo penetrates the apparent depth of clothing, conducting a kind of military strike against grime. In another essay, on the occasion of a plastics exhibition in Paris, Barthes notes how plastic is treated less as a material for making things than a miraculous embodiment of the human ability to transform nature into wholly domestic, wholly bourgeois objects of utility (MY: 97–9). Unlike more natural materials, such as wood, plastic objects are negative and have no other value than their use. Plastic offers up a vision of a human world in which all objects are transformed objects or, in other words, of human origin.

Plastic is a miraculous substance; it clearly demonstrates the human power over nature, and yet it is ultimately naturalized, filled with the self-image of a bourgeois culture which views itself as timeless and universal. In the same manner, wine, as a substance, is full of contradictions: sustenance for the worker, it is a sign of virility for the intellectual; in winter it apparently warms the drinker, in summer it apparently cools and refreshes; source of inebriation, wine, Barthes argues, is never associated in France with the desire for intoxication or with the causes of crime (MY: 58–61). All these contradictions can be sustained around the image of wine because ultimately wine signifies French identity. To drink wine is to be part of France, is to be French: 'to believe in wine is a coercive collective act' (MY: 59). This is the manner in which myths function in modern society, according to Barthes. Myth takes a purely cultural and historical object such as wine and transforms it into the sign of a universal value: here, the notion of a collective French identity. Wine comes to signify something, a comfortable, domesticated and yet social French cultural identity (*drink wine and be French!*), which hides the historical reality and tensions within and around the nation of France. Barthes concludes his essay by reminding us that, despite its mythology, wine is produced by the processes of colonialization, in countries such as Algeria which 'impose on the Muslims, on the very land of which they have been dispossessed, a crop of which they have no need, while they lack even bread. There are thus very engaging myths which are however not innocent' (MY: 61).

The lasting impression of Barthes's practice is captured here. Taking very common images and ideas of modern cultural life, Barthes does not simply expose the mythology behind them, but perhaps more importantly exposes the fact that we were somehow aware of the mythological character of such images and ideas all along. In his 'Ornamental Cookery' (MY: 78–80), for example, Barthes notes the manner in which glossy magazines such as *Elle*, marketed at mainly lower-class female audiences, present fantasy food in a glazed form (caramelized, oiled, embalmed and sheened). *Elle*, that is, presents food to be looked at (outside the readers' weekly budget), while *L'Express*, marketed at a higher wage-earning readership, presents real food: food to be bought and eaten. In a similar fashion, commenting on a Paris exhibition entitled 'The Great Family of Man' (MY: 100–2), Barthes notes how work is represented in the exhibition on the same level as birth and death. Thus, an exhibition supposedly demonstrating the diversity of human cultures ultimately homogenizes (essentializes) all humanity into a timeless and universal idea which denies the historical and cultural differences which make work an act of individual or collective agency in some cultures and an act of alienated labour under capitalism in others.

Mythology transforms one culture's values, in Barthes's case bourgeois French culture, into a universal and natural value: it turns culture into nature, often while still recognizing its status as myth, as a cultural product. It is this duplicity of myth, a construct which represents itself as universal and natural, which characterizes its ideological function. Barthes gives an example from a copy of *Paris-Match* offered to him at a barber's shop. The cover photograph shows a young black man in a French military uniform saluting, 'his eyes uplifted, probably fixed on a fold of the tricolour'. The reality of the photograph seems indisputable: this young black man is a French soldier caught here in a moment of time. There is, however, another meaning, which Barthes describes in terms of the idea: 'that France is a great Empire, that all her sons, without any colour discrimination, faithfully serve under her flag' (MY: 116). The ideological implication of the image, as described by Barthes, is unavoidable. And yet for those who want to deny the ideological and thus historically specific character of this idea of the all-inclusive French nation, for those who want to present that idea as indisputable, universal and even natural, there is always the possibility of simply invoking the image in its literal sense. How can one, after all, argue with a photograph: the camera, as people say (thus evoking another general myth), never lies. A similar phenomenon has occurred in the week in which I am writing this chapter. The British Queen Mother having died, thousands of people have decided to queue for hours to pass by her coffin as it lies in state. The British media is thus able to portray such a phenomenon, involving a tiny fraction of the British public, as proof of the abiding love of the whole of the British people for its monarchy. The British people, suggests the press and television coverage, are ultimately united, linked by common values and beliefs.

Frequently, the ideological meaning of such images does not need to be stated openly, since it is an ideology which requires little effort to reactivate. Barthes writes:

> The whole of France is steeped in this anonymous ideology: our press, our films, our theatre, our pulp literature, our rituals, our Justice, our diplomacy, our conversations, our remarks about the weather, a murder trial, a touching wedding, the cooking we dream of, the garments we wear, everything, in everyday life, is dependent on the representation which the bourgeoisie *has and makes us have* of the relations between man and the world. These 'normalized' forms attract little attention, by the very fact of their extension, in which their origin is easily lost.
>
> (MY: 140)

The role of the mythologist, therefore, is to expose, or often simply to remind us, of the artificial and constructed nature of such images. Barthes's project in *Mythologies* is to demystify myth. However, as we have just seen, myths are not simply delusions, tricks played upon us by those in positions of power. The cover image of *Paris-Match* suggests an ideology, and yet it is also simply a photograph of a real soldier. The British media makes an ideological point out of the long queues waiting to pass by the Queen Mother lying in state; yet the people in those queues exist and no doubt believe in and actually live that ideology themselves. There is a clear need for a more sophisticated model of meaning when confronting the numerous myths that make up a national culture. Such a model would need to be able to explain how an image, a filmed event, a court case, a sporting occasion, a routine piece of journalism, a building such as the Eiffel Tower or a construction such as the London Eye, can sustain and indeed propagate different and often conflicting levels of meaning. Such a model would need to explain how something can at one and the same time be literally itself and the medium through which ideology propagates itself. Barthes attempts to present such a model in his essay 'Myth Today', which demonstrates the profound impact on his work of the linguistic theories of Ferdinand de Saussure (1857–1913).

THE INFLUENCE OF SAUSSURE: SEMIOLOGY AND STRUCTURALISM

In a lecture given in Italy in 1974 Barthes states that he was first influenced by the theories of the Swiss linguist Ferdinand de Saussure in between completing the articles which make up *Mythologies* and writing the 'postface', 'Myth Today', which in 1957 was included with them (SC: 4–5). 'Myth Today', Barthes states there, was his first, euphoric reaction to a theory which promised to add a scientific rigour to the project he had so far pursued: the project of critiquing bourgeois culture. In this way he links the articles which make up *Mythologies* with earlier works such as *Writing Degree Zero* and represents 'Myth Today' as the beginning of a new phase of work focused on the idea of a science of criticism, more precisely structuralism and semiology.

What does Barthes mean by semiology? Sometimes referred to as *semiotics*, semiology is the general science of signs posited by Saussure in his lectures on linguistics published posthumously in 1915 as *Course in General Linguistics*. Saussure imagined a science that would be able to read systematically all human sign systems. Semiology is therefore frequently used to refer to the analysis of signs other than those found in linguistic sign systems. To understand semiology and what it does for Barthes at the end of his *Mythologies*, of course, we need to understand what Saussure means by a sign and, indeed, the theory of language out of which that definition of signs emerges.

Saussure's linguistic theories revolutionized the approach to language, formerly dominated by philology (the study of the history of words). The influence of these theories on Barthes comes from the development of structural linguistics in France and elsewhere in Europe, particularly after the Second World War. Structural linguistics takes up the approach to language laid down in Saussure's work. In that work Saussure takes language not as a historical phenomenon

SPEECH AND LANGUAGE

Saussure, in redefining linguistics, is faced with the problem that there is an infinity of actual and potential acts of language or speech. How could a linguist ever account for every act of language that occurs? Saussure's solution, the centre of his new linguistics, is to distinguish between speech or acts of language (parole) and language itself (la langue). All the numerous possible acts of language (parole) are created from a system (la langue). The language system (la langue) is comprised of the rules which make utterances (acts of language, parole) possible. Structural linguistics, after Saussure, studies the language system, its rules and codes, rather than studying speech, actual acts of language (parole).

but as a system existing in the present moment of time. The idea of language as a system presumes a distinction, in fact an opposition between speech and language.

The idea of structure enshrined in the name structuralism stems from this Saussurean differentiation between speech and language. When theorists such as Barthes refer to structure they are referring to the idea of a system (la langue) out of which utterances (parole) are generated. We might, therefore, refer to the *structure* of a literary text (out of which all the text's meanings are generated), but we can equally refer to the structure of literature as a whole, or the structure of the realist novel out of which all particular realist novels are generated. If we have signs, of whatever kind, then, according to Saussure and the structuralist movement after him, we must be dealing with an overall structure, a system (la langue). In structuralism, signs are understood in terms of the systems or structures which generate them. But we need, at this stage, to be slightly more specific about what a sign is. For Saussure, and structuralism after him, a sign is the product of an arbitrary (a conventional) relation between a signifier and a signified.

Semiology is the idea of a general study of the sign systems which make up our societies. Taking its cue from Saussure's model of linguistics, semiology should ultimately encompass linguistics, since language is merely one of the systems of signs which semiology will study. Semiology shares with structuralism a basis in Saussurean linguistics and its extension to other sign systems. Structuralism, as a

SIGN, SIGNIFIER, SIGNIFIED

Saussure redefines the relationship between language and the world through a new definition of words or the *sign*. Signs do not have their meaning because of a direct relationship with objects or actions in the world. A sign is the combination of a material *signifier* (sound or written mark) and a *signified* (concept). The signified is not the object or action but its mental concept. In English the combination of the sounds k + a + u (cow) is linked to the signified (the concept) cow ('the female of the domestic or any bovine animal'). In German, of course, it is the signifier *kuh* which performs this task; in French it is the signifier *vache*. The sign is arbitrary; it has meaning not directly in terms of the world, but in terms of its place in a language system (la langue). But language is merely one kind of sign system. There are numerous sign systems in our world, from the Highway Code to architectural design, from the clothes we wear to the food we eat. Everything in society is a sign in this sense and thus belongs to a system which, Saussure argues, can be studied like the system of language.

movement in post-war European thought, manifests itself in all the major disciplines of the Humanities and Social Sciences: literary study, sociology, history, anthropology, psychoanalysis, philosophy and, of course, linguistics. Believing that a focus on language (after Saussure) would bring such disciplines a greater objectivity and even scientific status, structuralism rejects more traditional Humanistic approaches to meaning and history by focusing on the rules and codes of structural systems rather than on the human subjects who work with and under such systems. Structuralism is, therefore, not concerned with the content (meaning) of utterances, such as individual literary texts, but with establishing the rules and codes (the system) which allow for the articulation of that content in the first place. Structuralism, as a critical approach, studies the system out of which literary texts emerge: it does not, therefore, study literary texts in and for themselves. Ultimately, structuralism and semiology as terms feed into each other and are thus difficult to define separately. In the work of Barthes, however, semiology is often reserved for his work on sign systems, whereas structuralism is more frequently employed in his analysis of literary narratives.

SEMIOLOGY AND MYTH

As a model of how meaning is produced, semiology contributes greatly to Barthes's project in *Mythologies*. It provides him with a clear and coherent explanation as to how myth does its work. The concept of the sign is crucial in this regard. In 'Myth Today' Barthes reminds us that the sign is, in fact, involved in a three-part relationship. A sign is, after all, the relation between a signifier and a signified, a sound or mark and a concept. The sign is the relation we draw between signifier and signified. If roses, for example, are a sign of romance in our culture, then they are so because, when used, say, in a love poem or pictured on a Valentine's Day card, they combine a signifier (the word or the image) with a signified (the cultural concept of roses) to produce the rose as a sign of romance, passion and love. The sign, then, is the equivalence we draw between a signifier and a signified. The relationship can be portrayed as shown in Figure 1.

There is one important difference between language, as described by Saussure, and the signs of myth, however; a difference which takes us back to our recognition of the duplicity or doubleness of such signs. The image of the black French soldier is on one level simply that, an image, a photograph. Yet, as we saw, it has another, ideological, mythic meaning which can be reduced to a phrase such as 'French patriotism' or even 'the inclusive, unified French nation'. The language studied by Saussure is a *first-order system*: it involves a signifier, a signified and their combination in a sign. Myth acts on already existent signs, whether they be written statements or texts, photographs, films, music, buildings or garments. The sign in the photograph of the black French soldier is

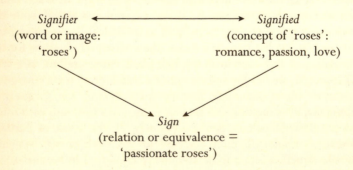

Signifier ⟷ *Signified*
(word or image: (concept of 'roses':
'roses') romance, passion, love)

Sign
(relation or equivalence =
'passionate roses')

Figure 1

already that, a sign. Mythology takes this sign and turns it into a signifier for a new signified, a new concept. As Barthes puts it: 'myth is a peculiar system, in that it is constructed from a semiological chain which existed before it: it *is a second-order semiological system*. That which is a sign (namely the associative total of a concept and an image) in the first system, becomes a mere signifier in the second' (MY: 114). A newspaper picture of crowds waiting to see the coffin of the Queen Mother is a first-order sign: signifier = the photographic image of crowds, signified = the crowds that waited to see the Queen Mother lying in state, sign = press reportage of a topical event which we might gloss as 'large crowds have queued for hours to see the Queen Mother lying in state'. Mythology raises the image to a second order level, however, turning that sign into a signifier for a new signified and thus a new sign: 'the unified, British public or nation or the British people's love of (acceptance of) the monarchy'. Barthes represents this relationship in the following manner (MY: 115), shown in Figure 2.

Myth, then, transforms first-order meanings into second-order meanings. Barthes explains by way of an example taken from the French writer Paul Valéry (MY: 115–16). The example is of a schoolboy who opens his Latin grammar book and reads the phrase *quia ego nominor leo*. The first-order meaning of the Latin phrase is obviously its literal meaning: 'because my name is lion'. However, it is clear that this meaning signifies something else, which Barthes paraphrases in the following way: 'I am a grammatical example meant to illustrate the rule about the agreement of the predicate' (MY: 116). Which is to say, the phrase is hardly there to convey something about the lion itself, but uses a first-order meaning to convey a second-order meaning concerning grammatical rules and conventions. If we switch from the

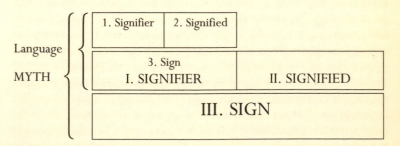

Figure 2

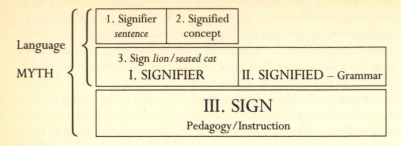

Figure 3

teaching of Latin to English grammar, we might think here of the rather more prosaic but certainly ubiquitous example of 'The cat sat on the mat.' We can chart the transformation involved in these examples as shown in Figure 3.

We now have a sense of how to read the duplicity or doubleness of myth. Myth, as it were, hijacks meaning and turns it into a second-order meaning or what Barthes calls *signification*. Signification here refers to the second-order sign, it is meaning which has been produced through the transformation of already existent meaning, already exist-ent (first-order) signs. Myth is a *metalanguage*: a second-order language which acts on a first-order language, a language which generates meaning out of already existent meaning. However, as Barthes also reminds us, the original, first-order meaning is not completely forgotten. A photograph of a young black soldier, although mythically signifying something about the French nation, can always also simply be seen as a photograph of a single individual. This is precisely why myth is so important to the perpetuation and dissemination of bour-geois ideology. Since the signifier of myth can always point towards two directions, it is maddeningly difficult to criticize. If we attempt to criticize the photograph of the young soldier in terms of its mythical propagation of French imperialism, its signifier can simply be turned towards the first-order literal meaning: one individual soldier salutes the flag. If we try to find out about the literal level of the photograph's meaning, we find that this level is emptied of all content, since the point is not the actual, individual soldier (his origins, beliefs, biography) but what he represents (or signifies). Myth, writes Barthes, acts like an alibi and says, always: 'I am not where you think I am; I am where you think I am not' (MY: 123). Thus, the *Paris-Match* image of the young soldier empties the history (the specificity) of that young man, transforming him into a type, an essence of French patriotism. Whatever way it turns its signifier (*this is a young man and nothing more, this is every French man and woman*), it evacuates the image of any real history and presents it as unquestionable, the essence of French society, a kind of nature. The promise of semiology, and the reason for Barthes's enthusiastic adoption of it, is that it seems to be able to bring myth to order, to read it and therefore to provide the basis for a viable critique.

We must be careful at this point, however. At the end of 'Myth Today' Barthes returns to a theme which is familiar to readers of *Writing Degree Zero* and his *Critical Essays*: the irrepressible power of absorption evidenced by bourgeois culture. The method of semiological analysis of myth practised by Barthes in *Mythologies* can be absorbed by bourgeois culture as easily as forms of avant-garde writing are absorbed into Literature. Indeed, as Andy Stafford notes, within a few years of the publication of *Mythologies* Barthes was being consulted by the Renault car company on a new advertising campaign and 'asked to write in *Marie-Claire* on the battle between two rival fashion designers' (Stafford 1998: 157). As Jonathan Culler puts it: 'demystification does not eliminate myth but, paradoxically, gives it greater freedom' (Culler 2002: 28). The only answer to this inexorable absorption of demystification or critique, of course, is to continue to change the manner in which it is produced and presented. As Barthes pursues the promise of semiological analysis in his work of the 1960s, he also continually shifts his terminology and offers not a fixed model but always a beginning, a prospect, a prelude to a science which must change and mutate if it is to retain any potential for critique.

SEMIOLOGY, LINGUISTICS AND FASHION

The willingness to change, adapt and even radically revise the model of semiology received from Saussure can be immediately registered in Barthes's *Elements of Semiology*, an introductory study, first published in 1964 in the journal *Communications*. Barthes begins by noting that Saussure 'thought that linguistics merely formed a part of the general science of signs' (ESe: 77); semiology, that is, would eventually subsume linguistics. There is, however, Barthes argues, no escaping language: 'to perceive what a substance signifies is inevitably to fall back

on the individuation of a language: there is no meaning which is not des-
ignated, and the world of signifieds is none other than that of language'
(ESe: 78). While semiology is best defined as the study of signs other
than those of language, it cannot, Barthes argues, escape from the linguistic model, since it is in that model that we find the most compelling
and comprehensive account of what signs are and how they work.
Furthermore, semiological systems invariably rely at some point on language, whether that reliance involves a caption added to a photograph
in a newspaper or magazine, a utilization in advertisements or political
presentations of certain clichés or stereotypical statements, or the more
complex transformations from first-order to second-order meanings we
have just studied.

The most significant example of Barthes's reversal of Saussure's hierarchy, the subsumption of semiology into what Barthes in his *Elements
of Semiology* calls a 'trans-linguistics', comes in his most extensive semiological study, *Système de la Mode*, translated as *The Fashion System*.
Researched and written between 1957 and 1963, *The Fashion System* was
finally published in 1967. By then Barthes had begun to radically question the semiological system he had described in 'Myth Today', *Elements
of Semiology* and in other essays of the period. *The Fashion System* is
offered, then, as evidence of an approach that has already mutated into
something else; as a 'certain history of semiology' (FS: ix). Barthes
explains that while his initial objective was to study 'actual Fashion
(apprehended in clothing as worn or at least as photographed)' (FS: x),
he has actually focused merely on fashion as it is written. This might at
first seem a poor alternative to a semiological study of actual fashion.
Reducing fashion to the captions or little bits of text added to fashion
photographs in a very limited set of women's magazines (mainly *Elle*
and *Le Jardin des Modes*) in one particular fashion year (1958–9, from
June to June) will inevitably appear just that, a huge reduction of what
we mean by fashion. And yet, as much of Barthes's study is concerned
to demonstrate, this is precisely how the fashion system works: it passes
real garments through a series of structures until it finally meets the
public with a meaning, a sign, which is thoroughly linguistic, thoroughly
dependent upon language. Barthes asks rhetorically: 'Is there any
system of objects . . . which can dispense with articulated language? Is
not speech the inevitable relay of any signifying order?' (FS: xi).

The reversal of the Saussurean model is a propitious one in this
study, since Barthes, faced with fashion writing, can produce a sustained

analysis of the 'myths' that underpin and naturalize the fashion system. The fashion industry, after all, depends greatly on a series of 'myths' in order to produce an innocent façade which, in fact, acts to speed up consumption. That is to say, without a mythology of clothing people might well be happy to exist within 'the slow time of wear' (FS: xii). Clothes, generally, take a long time to wear out. The myths of the fashion system exist to speed up consumption, to lock people (women in the main) into an annual system which can generate consumption through a vocabulary of interchangeable, layered and repeatable functions.

Fashion statements come down, Barthes argues, to a simple formula, or what he terms a matrix, which can be described in terms of an Object of signification, a Support of signification and a Variant (O, S, V). Thus 'skirts with a full blouse' can be represented in the following way (FS: 64):

skirts with a full blouse
O   V   S

The point about both the Variant (V) and the Support of signification (S) is that once they are established in one example we can immediately start thinking about alternative examples. Thus:

skirts with a half blouse
O   V   S

or

skirts with a denim blouse
O   V   S

or

skirts with a see-through blouse
O   V   S

Clearly, one of the chief features of this formula (or matrix) is that it is so eminently repeatable. Once a successful formula has been established, it can be revised again and again with the simplest of adjustments to the Variant or the Support of signification. We should also note that

the distribution of O, V and S can be changed around: to take some
examples (FS: 73):

a cardigan with its collar open
    O   S   V

high waists for (evening) gowns
V   S   O

collars that are small for (sports) shirts
S   V   O

We should also note here the possibility of layered *matrices*, such as
(FS: 73):

$$\overbrace{\text{a matched ensemble, straw-hat and cache-peigne}}$$

$$\underbrace{\quad S_1 \qquad\qquad S_2 \qquad\qquad\qquad S_3 \quad}$$

$$\qquad V \qquad\qquad\qquad\qquad\qquad O$$

and that there is even the possibility of containing the Object of signification, the Support of signification and the Variant in a single word
(FS 77):

This year blue is in Fashion

This year's Fashion $\equiv$ $\overbrace{\text{(colour) blue}}$

                                      OS   V

The fashion system, on such a basis, can then be understood in terms
of a yearly changing of the Variant. Dresses remain each year, obviously, but their Variant, whether they are long or short, pleated or
tapered, closed with a zip or with buttons, allows the fashion system
to perpetually recreate and regenerate its messages from a simple stock
of elements.

Barthes spends a great deal of time distinguishing between the different structures involved in the fashion system. The semiologist, faced with this system, is, after all, confronted with a 'real garment', the visual representation of garments and the 'written garment'. Many of the problems faced by Barthes when reading the fashion system concern the fact that he is dealing with multiple structures. His solution is to employ approaches from linguistics to demonstrate how levels of meaning build up messages which signify something either about the world (A-ensembles) or Fashion itself (B-ensembles). A statement such as 'Prints are winning at the races', for example, gives us an A-ensemble in that it not only says what is currently fashionable, but also provides us with an image of social power. A statement such as 'Women will shorten skirts to the knee, adopt pastel checks, and wear two-toned pumps', however, functions more as a direct statement of what is fashionable and thus is an example of a B-ensemble.

Using a distinction that is important throughout his work, Barthes states that fashion in A-ensembles is a *connoted* value (one infers that wearing a printed dress at social events will make one fashionable), whereas fashion is a *denoted* value in B-ensembles.

Fashion writing, Barthes demonstrates, works by building up chains of *combinations* (indicated thus '●') and *equivalences* (indicated thus '≡') which take a large set of elements and build basic messages out of them. We are extremely familiar with such processes within the world of advertising, a world in which such combinations and equivalences are the stock techniques by which a huge array of products are presented and sold to us. Combine a brand of lager with the idea of Alpine skiing and the result will be the production of an equivalence: coolness, sophistication, refreshment, active masculinity. The possibilities, as those who work within the world of advertising know, are endless. Thus, faced with a statement such as 'daytime clothes in town are accented with white', Barthes can reconstruct the set of equivalences and combinations in the following way: 'daytime clothes ● accents ● white ≡ city'. This then allows us to reconstruct the following proposition: 'White accents on daytime clothes are the sign of the city' (FS: 48). The various levels or codes of the fashion system, therefore, work by turning signifieds into signifiers for new signifieds. Here, for example, what looks like a statement of fact on one level (signified = 'daytime clothes in town are accented with white') becomes a signifier for a new signified at another level (signified = 'White accents on

DENOTATION AND CONNOTATION

In *Elements of Semiology* Barthes takes up the distinction, developed by the linguist Louis Hjelmslev (1899–1965), between denotation and connotation. A denotative statement is a first-order statement: a statement which concerns the literal (first-order) meaning of the words that make up that statement. When faced with the statement 'Prints are winning at the races', for example, we have the words used, or what Barthes calls a *plane of expression* (E), we have what the words literally mean, or the *plane of content* (C), and we then draw a *relation* between the two (R) to find the statement's meaning. On the level of denotation, 'Prints are winning at the races' is a rather strange statement. Does this statement seriously expect us to believe that its meaning involves printed clothes and the winning of horse races? If we simply expect to find the meaning by moving from

(E)   *plane of expression* (words used/selected: 'Prints are winning at the races')

to

(C)   *plane of content* (literal meaning of the statement 'Prints are winning at the races'),

then we will be disappointed. Simply moving from (E) to (C) here gives us a nonsensical first-order (denotative) meaning. We need to move to the relation (R) between (E) and (C), and thus to a second-order meaning (connotation) to make any sense of the statement. There is clearly another meaning implied in this statement and this meaning exists at the level of connotation. To move from the plane of denotation to connotation involves the same processes we have already seen in the reading of myth: we move from a first-order meaning (denotation) to a second-order meaning (connotation). In our example the connotation involves a statement about what is fashionable and also an analogy between being fashionable (wearing prints) and power (winning, being seen as a winner). Barthes expresses the relation in the following manner (ESe: 149):

```
2   E     R     C
1   ERC
```

As Barthes puts it: *'the first system (ERC) becomes the plane of expression, or signifier, of the second system'* and thus can also be expressed: (ERC) R C. As Barthes adds: 'the first system is then the plane of *denotation* and the second system (wider than the first) the plane of *connotation*. We shall therefore say that a *connoted system is a system whose plane of expression is itself constituted by a signifying system'* (ibid.). Connotation, an implied, second-order, plane of meaning will continue to be of enormous importance in Barthes's structuralist, and indeed his post-structuralist, phases.

daytime clothes are the sign of the city'). As we proceed through these levels we enter more thoroughly into the realm of connotation or connotative meaning. Ultimately, however, the signified of the statement we are looking at here signifies something else than is literally, denotatively contained in its expression and content. An image of modernity, the urban or metropolitan, or of hygiene or simplicity is ultimately at stake in the statement. How we respond to this last level of signification, which Barthes styles in terms of the 'rhetorical code', will depend on the context of the magazine or journal in which the statement is presented.

The rhetorical code involves the world-view or the ideological signs which such examples of the fashion system wishes its readers to accept. Barthes's study of the fashion system ultimately leads, therefore, to a reconstruction and analysis of the 'myths' which are the end-product of such complex sign systems. Fashion works in ways already familiar to readers of Barthes's *Mythologies*: it either hides its meanings behind the appearance of utility or naturalness (as in A-ensembles) or declares them as a kind of legal fact (as in B-ensembles) (FS: 263–4). Fashion, as a form of 'myth', converts the artificial into a sign of 'nature' and then hides the fact that it has performed this transformation (FS: 283–4).

Based on equivalences and combinations (between Fashion and the world, between clothing and Fashion), the fashion system, which we should remember is based on the decisions of a very small number of editors and consultants, ultimately presents such arbitrary relations as if they were inevitable, natural or a kind of inescapable law. As Barthes writes: 'it is obviously because Fashion is tyrannical and its signs arbitrary that it must convert its sign into a natural fact or a rational law' (FS: 263). In this sense, *The Fashion System* is the largest, most extensive and, perhaps, as Rick Rylance has suggested, the most depressing and pessimistic 'mythology' Barthes was ever to write (Rylance 1994: 42). It is also, however, Barthes's most devastatingly rigorous critique of bourgeois ideology and its tendency to naturalize the signs that it produces. As such, *The Fashion System* is a crucial stage in our understanding of the development of Barthes's thought in the 1960s and our sense of the link between his work on myth and social semiological systems and his work on the structural analysis of literary texts.

SUMMARY

In this chapter we have seen the manner in which Barthes extends the critique of bourgeois culture presented in his earlier work into a full-scale critical analysis of modern 'mythology'. Myth, a thoroughly ideological process, works by presenting culturally specific objects and relations as if they were timeless, natural, and thus unquestionable. Barthes employs semiology to establish a rigorous technique for the demythologizing of modern French culture's all-pervasive mythological meanings.

4

STRUCTURALISM

This chapter continues our analysis of Barthes's engagement with semiology and structuralism. Here we turn from Barthes's semiological analysis of modern sign systems to his involvement with the project to establish a structural account of narratives. Before reaching that important phase in Barthes's career, however, it is necessary to look at the manner in which his public image as a theorist and critic developed in the 1960s. Barthes is, in the 1960s, increasingly seen as a leading figure in a new form of literary criticism pitted directly against the kind of criticism practised within the major universities. It is important to look at the debate (sometimes styled a 'quarrel') which Barthes's work of the 1950s and 1960s helped to stimulate between conservative and avant-garde forms of criticism.

OLD AND NEW CRITICISM: 'THE PICARD AFFAIR'

What happens when Barthes begins to apply to literary criticism the kind of theories we have looked at in the last chapter? The first answer we must give is that it produces controversy. In various essays in which Barthes first registers the impact of semiology and structuralism on his thinking, he makes a distinction between what he calls 'the two criticisms' (CE: 249–54). One kind of criticism is new, embracing the emergent models and approaches stemming from structuralism, psychoanalysis and other theoretical developments. Barthes styles this kind of criticism as interpretive. It is a kind of criticism which displays openly its attachment to ideological positions (Marxist, Existentialist, Psychoanalytical) and it does so because it performs the fundamental critical task of reflecting on itself, its own language, its own relation to the object of study. In contrast to interpretive criticism, Barthes refers to what he calls academic criticism, and at other times 'Lansonism', after the Sorbonne Professor Gustave Lanson who laid the ground-rules for literary criticism in France in the first half of the twentieth century. Academic criticism pretends it is outside of ideology and makes the mistake of trying to find the meaning of literary works in their authors and also in other external contexts, such as historical or biographical events. Barthes came back to such themes in *On Racine*, contrasting his interpretive work on Racine to the traditional, academic approach.

Barthes's critique of academic criticism involves a complicated social and political map of university institutions in Paris and France generally (see Bourdieu 1988). Barthes, we should remember, by the 1960s was working in the École Prâtique des Hautes Études (EPHE), an institution favourably disposed to the new semiological and structuralist ideas: by 1962 Barthes was director of studies of the 'sociology of signs, symbols and representations' in the EPHE (Calvet 1994: 135). His attack on academic criticism was therefore surely meant to refer to more traditional seats of learning. Certainly, the Sorbonne Professor of French Literature and renowned Racine scholar, Raymond Picard, took it that way. Picard's 1964 pamphlet *New Criticism or New Fraud?* attacked Barthes directly and labelled what Picard called the new criticism as confused, obscurantist and ultimately disrespectful of literary greatness. The debate between Picard and Barthes made national and international news and certainly helped to increase Barthes's reputation as a major representative of avant-garde theory and criticism in contemporary France. It also prompted Barthes to one of the clearest expressions of his vision of literary criticism.

Criticism and Truth, first published in 1966, is Barthes's answer to Picard. Since Picard had labelled a quite diverse and, according to Barthes, heterogeneous collection of critics and theorists as 'new', Barthes provocatively labels Picard's approach as 'l'ancienne critique' ('old criticism') (see *Œuvres complètes*, Vol. 2: 20). What 'old criticism' cannot stand, Barthes argues, is that 'new criticism' concerns itself not with critical evaluation (the foundation of traditional forms of criticism) but with language itself. Focusing on language shatters a number of 'old critical' rules, in particular the rule of 'verisimilitude', that is that criticism should rely on traditional, established values. Barthes's argument here clearly relates to his critique of 'common sense' in *Mythologies* and elsewhere, and strives to demonstrate the naturalizing intentions of critics such as Picard. The 'old critical' rules of 'objectivity', 'good taste' and 'clarity' of language all serve, Barthes contends, to keep literature safe, to protect it from ideology, from history and ultimately from symbolic language, which cannot be reduced to singular meanings. Old criticism, Barthes argues, wants to present itself as disinterested, in the sense of outside, or beyond, ideological concerns. Such a position, however, is betrayed by old criticism's reliance on the bourgeois ideology of common sense, objectivity, good taste and clarity. Its emphasis on clarity, for example, is merely a way of labelling as 'jargon' any critical discourse it dislikes. Barthes, in his *Mythologies*, had already produced a telling account of such a practice in an essay entitled 'Blind and Dumb Criticism', in which he had noted the manner in which bourgeois criticism frequently allowed itself a certain incomprehension when faced with ideas it wished to reject. When confronted with Existentialism or Marxism, for example, bourgeois criticism's reaction is often to say: 'I don't understand, therefore you are idiots' (MY: 35). Old criticism, in this sense, acts in bad faith, in that it hides its ideological presuppositions. Moreover, in performing such a practice, it abnegates its responsibility as criticism, which is to deal with ideas. If one thing unites the 'new criticism', Barthes argues, it is its recognition of the need for criticism to display its attachment to the available ideological positions, be they Existentialist, psychoanalytic, Marxist or conservative.

Criticism and Truth moves beyond Picard to present an analysis of what it means for criticism to concern itself with language. Barthes here describes three attitudes towards the literary text: science, criticism and reading. The scientific approach is the structuralist approach which concerns itself with the general system (the 'hypothetical model of description') out of which literary works can be generated. This kind of criticism is a science of literature which has nothing to say about the content of individual works, concentrating as it does on the conditions which make meaning possible. The clearest example of this approach concerns a project to which Barthes was a major contributor, centred as it was within the EPHE, which attempted to lay the foundations for a structuralist analysis of narratives. Barthes's 'Introduction to the Structural Analysis of Narratives' (SC: 95–135; also IMT: 79–124 and BSW: 251–95) is his now classic contribution to that project.

THE STRUCTURAL ANALYSIS OF NARRATIVES

Barthes begins his 'Introduction to the Structural Analysis of Narratives' with the characteristic first move of any structural analysis, a move we are now quite familiar with. Barthes begins by reminding us that narrative is as old as human civilization and that, therefore, there are simply countless narratives which could be analysed. Faced with such an infinity of narratives, how does anyone ever begin to analyse them? The answer is the same as that given by Saussure when faced with the countless examples of language in the world, or when Barthes is faced with the numerous examples of actual fashion. We cannot begin with actual examples of narrative, or language, or fashion. A structural analysis, like Saussure's in his structural linguistics, must disregard *parole* (acts of narrative, of language, or of fashion) and must move immediately to the construction of a 'hypothetical model' (SC: 97). The analysis of narrative, if it is to be scientific, must change from an inductive approach (extrapolating meaning from individual examples) to a deductive approach (establishing a working model against which to test all individual examples). The most relevant and viable model available, Barthes argues, is that of language and therefore of structural linguistics. The rationale for such a move comes from the structuralist argument that all acts of narrative (parole) must come from a system of codes and conventions (la langue): 'no one can combine (produce) a narrative without referring to an implicit system of units and rules' (SC: 97).

The structural analysis of narratives models itself, therefore, on linguistics. In fact, Barthes argues, it draws a homology (correspondence) between narrative and the sentence. Linguistics, Barthes notes, stops at the sentence; it takes the sentence as its highest term and proceeds to study all the rules of combination and opposition which allow for sentences to be constructed. Narratives, of course, are much larger than sentences, they contain many sentences. Narratives are a kind of discourse, discourse here being understood as the broad categories of linguistic representation in society: narrative, poetry, intellectual/

SYNTAGMATIC AND PARADIGMATIC

The syntagmatic and paradigmatic (sometimes called the *systematic*, sometimes the *associative*) axes of language demonstrate a point made by Saussure that language works through relations of combination and association (see Jefferson and Robey 1986: 49–51). A simple sentence, such as 'Prints are winning at the races', relies on two axes. The sentence works by a horizontal spacing or sequential arrangement of the words one after the other (the *syntagmatic axis*). This sequential combination of words obeys the rules of grammar (Main Verb after Subject, Object after Main Verb). The sentence, however, is also constructed through a series of choices. There are, for example, a number of words that could be chosen instead of the word 'winning': 'triumphant', 'victorious', 'first' or 'first home', and, of course, in the context from which Barthes takes the sentence, 'fashionable'. This is the vertical, associative level of language: the *associative* or *paradigmatic axis*. Sentences work, then, by combining words in sequences, but those words have the meaning they do because they are associated with other words. Sentences work because they combine words (syntagmatic axis) but also because they choose certain words at the expense of others (paradigmatic axis). Barthes discusses the two axes of language in *Elements of Semiology* (see ESe: 121–48).

philosophical prose. To construct the model (system) of narratives, however, we have to treat narratives as if they were a single unit like a sentence (SC: 99). What this homology (correspondence) between sentence and narrative allows Barthes and other structuralists to do is to incorporate into their study of narratives a host of principles culled from linguistics. The most important example, perhaps, is the basic linguistic opposition between the *syntagmatic* and the *paradigmatic* axes of language.

In a manner corresponding to the syntagmatic and paradigmatic axes of language, Barthes's structural analysis of narratives focuses on the way in which sequential levels, such as the actions involved in a narrative, are integrated into higher levels of meaning. There are three levels of narrative, Barthes argues: a basic level of primary units, which Barthes calls *functions*; a higher level, which Barthes calls the level of Actions: one final, highest level, which Barthes calls the level of Narrative itself. Thus, we get:

Narrative

Actions

functions.

To read narratives in a structural manner is to demonstrate the manner in which narrative meaning is generated by a process of integration, functions being integrated into Actions and Actions finally being integrated at the level of Narrative itself.

Functions include all elements of narrative, since, as Barthes claims, there is nothing which does not have a meaning in a narrative text. Even the most trivial function in a narrative, such as a telephone ringing, or the lighting of a cigarette, has meaning (SC: 104). Barthes divides functions into two sorts. *Distributive functions* involve a kind of cause and effect logic: if a telephone rings it will either be answered or not. We find the meaning of such functions in what comes immediately after them. Contrasted to distributive functions come another type which Barthes calls *indices*: these are details which can be collected together and help to produce a kind of meaning that is not essentially chronological; they can contribute, for example, to what we would call 'character'. These functions, such as noting the colour of a character's hair, or the fact that it suddenly begins to rain when a particular character enters the street, are only understandable by moving to the next level of Actions. Indices are thus integrated at a higher level. For example, what we call the 'character' in a narrative ('character' may be describable through one word, such as 'evil' or 'dangerous' or 'saintly' or 'virginal') is never named directly but usually is indexed through a host of functional details: the clothes they wear, the manner in which they talk, walk, eat their dinner, treat their pets or their parents and so on. Ian Fleming's famous secret agent, James Bond (Ian Fleming's *Goldfinger* is Barthes's example in this essay), for example, is surrounded by a host of such indices, none of which can be understood unless we integrate them into larger groupings on the level of Actions.

The manner in which we perform such an integrative movement, ultimately for both functions and indices, allows Barthes to introduce some of the most important structuralist ideas and thinkers into his analysis. Barthes, for example, refers to the work of Vladimir Propp (1895–1970) who had produced detailed classifications of kinds of *sequences* in folk tales. A sequence, as used by Propp and adapted by Barthes here, collects a number of functions into Actions which are recognizable under certain conventional names: Fraud, the Betrayal, Seduction, Conflict (SC: 114–15). It should not be difficult to understand how fairy tales, for example, rely on a highly repetitive use of sequences: ending with a marriage between the hero and the heroine, for example, is invariable in such tales, as is the presence in one form or another of an evil figure intent on stopping such a happy, matrimonial ending. To recognize sequences and to name them on a general level is to have integrated a series of functions into the level of Actions. Far from presenting us with a unique narrative, a folk tale, as studied by Propp, works by reactivating very well-known sequences and thus easily moving us as readers from the particularities of the tale to the conventional meanings (the Actions) which that tale rehearses once again. Similarly, we can perform such a grouping and naming around the indices which signify character-roles; Barthes employs A.J. Greimas's (1917–92) six basic character-roles (Subject and Object, Giver and Receiver, Helper and Opponent) (SC: 119), while recognizing that, in modern novels, there are many other kinds of possible names for character-roles, such as the beloved, the suitor, the betrayer, the seducer and so on.

As Barthes notes, such structural procedures begin to offer up the possibility of a scientific description of different kinds of narratives. Folk tales, for example, as studied by Propp, rely heavily on simple functions and the sequences they generate. Character is not greatly emphasized in such narratives. On the other hand, modern novels seem very reliant on the *indexing* of character, generating through that process the complex 'psychological realism' so typical of such forms of narrative.

Narratives, as the above comments demonstrate, do not directly represent reality. Barthes's engagement with the structural analysis of narratives is a key moment in his life-long critique of the bourgeois ideal of literary realism, a critique we have already observed in his first work, *Writing Degree Zero*. The modern novel uses functions and indices of character and atmosphere to generate the illusion of 'reality'. As Barthes frequently notes, in bourgeois Literature that which is detailed (in terms of description) is always associated with 'reality', with 'realism'. Barthes's engagement with the structural analysis of narratives continues, therefore, his demystification of bourgeois Literature by demonstrating the systematic (formal) rather than realistic basis of modern narratives. An abiding influence on Barthes in this respect is the structural anthropology of Claude Lévi-Strauss (1908–). Lévi-Strauss's influence on the structuralist movement in and outside of France is immense and stems from his application of structuralist principles to the study of primitive cultures. In works such as *Structural Anthropology* (1950), *The Savage Mind* (1962) and *The Raw and the Cooked* (1964), Lévi-Strauss moved anthropology away from a study of the content or specific meaning of the rituals and myths of primitive societies towards a structural understanding of general systems of signification which could then also be related to apparently more civilized societies. As Barthes states, in his 1962 essay on Lévi-Strauss, 'Sociology and Socio-Logic': 'it is because society, any society, is concerned immediately to structure reality that structural analysis is necessary' (SC: 162). The implication of such a recognition, already registered in works like *Mythologies* and *The Fashion System*, is that all human practices in society are mediated, that is they are always already contained within systems of signification. Narrative fiction, in other words, never reaches us without having already gone through a process of signification. Narratives do not reach us directly and do not directly represent the world; their meaning is always bound up in a system (outlined here in Barthes's essay) which forms the basis of their meaning. The meaning of a narrative, in other words, stems from the system of narratives out of which it is produced and not from its representation of reality. The meaning of all narratives is mediated, understanding mediation here in its technical sense: that which passes through a process or system of transformation in its representation.

The mediated nature of narratives is particularly evident when we move to the highest level of the system, the level of Narrative itself. Just as sentences presume an 'I' (addresser) and a 'You' (an addressee), so, Barthes argues, narratives ultimately have to be understood in terms of how they posit a narrator and a reader. The traditional manner in which literary criticism has read the 'signs of the narrator' has been to posit an author behind them. Yet the idea of an author as the source of a narrative's signs runs directly against structural analysis, in that it suggests that a narrative's form and meaning stems from an original human consciousness. The idea of the author, in other words, suggests that narratives are not mediated but rather are unique expressions of unique authorial consciousnesses. As Barthes's famous essay 'The Death of the Author' (1968) reiterates, structural analysis must dispense with the author completely, reading the signs of narration and of reading purely within the system of narrative itself. As Barthes puts it: 'the psychological person (referential order) has no relation with the linguistic person, never defined by arrangements, intentions, or features, but only by (coded) place within the discourse' (SC: 125). Thus, Barthes asserts that the signs of the narrator follow the rules of language itself, presenting themselves, just as sentences must, either in the personal or the impersonal mode. Likewise, the signs of the reader concern the codes and practices by which narratives are received by society. Such codes and practices begin to take us outside of the narrative itself and into the various social situations in which narratives are received. Although this essay does not really develop this issue, Barthes does once again remark on the manner in which bourgeois Literature, particularly in the form of the realist novel, strives to conceal the signs of its social consumption. In this way, Barthes's structural analysis of narratives returns, eventually, to the demystifying project which we have been examining throughout this, and the last, chapter. As Barthes puts it: 'The reluctance to parade its codes marks bourgeois society and the mass culture which has issued from it: each demands signs which do not seem to be signs' (SC: 128).

'Introduction to the Structural Analysis of Narratives' represents Barthes's most famous and one of his most sustained attempts to demonstrate what he means by a science of literature. We need to remember, however, that such a *science* is one of three responses to the text posited by Barthes in *Criticism and Truth*. What about the responses Barthes terms criticism and reading? Barthes's work at the end of the 1960s and beginning of the 1970s begins to orient itself decisively towards these latter terms.

SUMMARY

In the period usually classified as his structuralist phase (1957–67) we find Barthes gaining notoriety as one of the leading figures of the 'new criticism'. The 'Picard Affair' prompted Barthes, in *Criticism and Truth* and elsewhere, to a clear articulation of his approach to criticism. This definition is important since it makes it clear that the drive to develop a structuralist science of literature is one, but only one, aspect of Barthes's agenda. In this chapter we have paid special attention to this structuralist aspect of Barthes's work in the 1960s. Structural linguistics offers the prospect of a science of literature, which Barthes applies in particular to the study of narratives. This scientific approach complements Barthes's work in semiology in that it demystifies traditional notions of meaning. Semiology and structuralist literary criticism both contribute, in Barthes's hands, to a critique of modern society through the demonstration of its frequently concealed reliance on artificial sign systems.

5

THE DEATH OF
THE AUTHOR

This chapter, along with the next, deals with Barthes's work from the late 1960s to the early 1970s. Culturally and politically, this period of French history is dominated by the student and workers' revolt of 1968 and its aftermath. In early May 1968, student protests against the Vietnam War and the rigidities of French politics (exemplified by the President, Charles de Gaulle) spread from Nanterre to the Sorbonne, to the streets of Paris and to other cities in France. The involvement of workers' unions and eventually the PCF and various left and far-left groups threatened, for a brief moment at the end of the month, to topple the government. Although the events of May 1968 were eventually contained by conventional political mechanisms, the spirit of radical, at times revolutionary, ideas came to dominate intellectual thought in France and beyond. The radical political events of the late 1960s are matched in France by the emergence of radical ideas associated with theorists and philosophers such as Jacques Derrida (1930–), Julia Kristeva (1941–), Michel Foucault (1926–84), Jean Baudrillard (1929–) and Philippe Sollers (1936–) among others. These new ideas have subsequently been grouped under the rather broad category of post-structuralism. Barthes's work of this period was greatly influenced by post-structuralist ideas and, in turn, was a significant influence on many of its seminal thinkers.

BEYOND SCIENCE: A NEW SEMIOLOGY

Even during the period of his greatest engagement with structuralism and semiology, from 'Myth Today' (1957) to the publication of *The Fashion System* (1967), Barthes had made it clear that the idea of a scientific study of sign systems, whether they be literary texts or cultural objects, was just that, an 'idea'. In *Criticism and Truth*, for example, when discussing structuralism as a 'science of literature', Barthes had been careful to present his comments in the future tense. As he explains in a 1971 interview with Stephen Heath:

> in *Critique et Vérité*, I did speak of a science of literature, but it was in general overlooked – to my dismay, because I formulated my sentence so that this would be seen by those who pay attention to ambiguities and ellipses – that in speaking of a science of literature I had put in parentheses: 'if it exists one day'; which meant that I did not in fact believe that discourse on literature could ever become 'scientific.'
>
> (GV: 131)

Elsewhere, Barthes has spoken of his structuralist phase as one in which he indulged in a temporary obsession for creating categories and classifications, a certain pleasure in exercising a 'Systematics' (SC: 6), as he puts it. In this sense, Barthes represents himself in the early to mid-1960s as a writer with similar credentials to the three authors studied in his 1971 book, *Sade/Fourier/Loyola*. In that text, Barthes brings together three extraordinarily different writers: the Marquis de Sade (1740–1814), infamous as an author of pornographic literature; Ignatius Loyola (1491–1556), founder of the Jesuit Order and author of the *Spiritual Exercises*; and Charles Fourier (1772–1837), author of politically utopian literature. What such diverse authors share, argues Barthes, is an obsession with system and classification. Sade classifies sexual acts, Loyola classifies spiritual acts and Fourier classifies social acts in his imaginary society of total harmony. Each of them is a 'founder of language', more concerned with the world created in their texts than representing the actual world around them (SFL: 6–7). Barthes the structuralist could also be read as a 'founder of language', generating a world (of classifications and systematic relations) in his texts. We might view Barthes, in his structuralist phase, as another lover of classifications, as obsessed as Sade, Fourier and

Loyola were with the pleasure produced by classification in and for its own sake.

As we have seen, however, it is entirely consistent with his own motives as a writer and theorist that Barthes should begin to challenge and even dismantle structuralist and semiological methods at the very moment they are beginning to be assimilated by a general academic and intellectual audience. This change in focus is succinctly discussed in an essay of 1971 in which Barthes looks back at what has changed since the publication of *Mythologies*. The essay is entitled 'Mythology Today' (RL: 65–8); it is also published as 'Change the Object Itself: Mythology Today' in *Image-Music-Text* (IMT: 165–9). What has not changed, of course, is the reliance of French culture on myths. However, as Barthes notes, the kind of demystifying reading of myths which he practised in *Mythologies* has become widespread and, in fact, assimilated by general culture, so that: 'any student can denounce the bourgeois or petit-bourgeois character of a form (of life, of thought, of consumption) . . . demystification (or demythification) has itself become a discourse, a corpus of phrases, a catechistic statement' (RL: 66). We saw in Chapter 3 how quickly Barthes's method in *Mythologies* was assimilated by cultural forces wholly dependent on the production of myth.

Semiology, and we can add structuralism, is in the position of writing as defined in Barthes's first book: it is threatened, if it does not regularly change itself, by a general and irreversible acculturation. Barthes's solution in 'Mythology Today' is to suggest a switch from the demystification of myths to a radical critique and dismantling of the very notion of the sign itself: 'it is no longer the myths which must be unmasked . . . but the sign itself which must be perturbed' (RL: 66). Such a change in focus involves a new kind of semiology with a new set of criteria. The task for this new semiology, writes Barthes, is 'no longer merely to *reverse* (or to *correct*) the mythic message, putting it right side up, with denotation at the bottom and connotation at the top, nature on the surface and class interest deep down, but to change the object itself' (RL: 68). The new object of demystification, Barthes argues, must be the sign itself: 'initially, we sought the destruction of the (ideological) signified; now we seek the destruction of the sign' (RL: 67).

Why must this new semiology, posited by Barthes in this essay, attack the sign itself? Surely, such a move would be contradictory to the very nature of semiology: the general study or science of signs in culture. Certainly, the idea of the sign, formerly the basis upon which semiology and structuralism established themselves as methods, seems to have undergone a remarkable change in this essay, appearing now as the arch-enemy. Barthes, indeed, seems now to be equating the sign with the very thing (bourgeois society) which it (the sign) formerly allowed him to critique. The object of critique for this new semiology, writes Barthes:

> is no longer French society, but far beyond it, historically and geographically, the whole of Western (Greco–Judeo–Islamo–Christian) civilization, unified in one and the same theology (essence, monotheism) and identified by the system of meaning it practices, from Plato to *France-Dimanche*.
>
> (RL: 67)

The sign must be attacked, it seems, because it is involved in a 'system of meaning' which underpins Western culture, from its philosophical origins (Plato and Greek philosophy) to its modern system of mass communication (here exemplified by the popular magazine *France-Dimanche*) and because it is somehow connected to philosophies and monotheistic religions which seek or believe that they embody the Truth. What have the Western tradition of philosophy and the major monotheistic religions got in common, and what does such a constellation share with modern mass communications? Why has Barthes conflated his lifelong critique of bourgeois French culture with an attack on the manner in which philosophy and the major monotheistic religions employ the sign?

DESTRUCTION OF THE SIGN: THE INFLUENCE OF DERRIDA

Barthes's points in 'Mythology Today' are very close to those made in the deconstructive philosophy of Jacques Derrida. Derrida published three extremely influential texts in 1967: *Speech and Phenomenon*, *Writing and Difference* and, most importantly of all, *Of Grammatology*. These texts were to be the basis of what has become known as deconstruction.

Barthes and Derrida, along with many other theorists associated with post-structuralism, took part in a major symposium at Johns Hopkins

University in 1966 on 'The Languages of Criticism and the Sciences of Man' (see Macksey and Donato 1972). The symposium is often cited as the moment at which a new post-structuralist tone begins to be heard within the structuralist movement. Derrida's contribution to the symposium, 'Structure, Sign and Play in the Discourse of the Human Sciences', is a crucial early expression of post-structuralism in general and deconstruction in particular (Derrida 1981: 278–93; also in Macksey and Donato 1972: 247–72). In this paper Derrida looks at the idea of structure itself. The idea of structure, Derrida reminds us, is not only an important one for structuralism, it has had a crucial role to play in all systems of thought since the beginning of the philosophical tradition. All ideas of structure, Derrida argues, depend upon the notion of a centre, an origin or foundation from which meaning flows. To take the example of literary works, the centre has traditionally been seen as the author: the source of all meaning, the origin from which the literary work derives. If we treat the literary work as

DECONSTRUCTION

Deconstruction has, since the early writings of Jacques Derrida, been a significant influence in all areas of the Humanities and beyond. Usually associated with a disruption of traditional oppositions (or *binary* oppositions) – man/woman, speech/writing, philosophy/literature, truth/fiction, outside/inside, form/content and so on – Derrida's work begins with a new analysis of the Saussurean sign. Saussure had seen the sign as comprising a signifier (sound or mark) and a signified (concept). The relation between signifier and signified, however, is an arbitrary one: it is only current convention (the language system as it currently operates) which connects the signifier with a particular signified. Saussure had noted that 'in language there are only differences without positive terms', by which he means that the relation between signifier and signified is purely structural, purely relational. The signified is not a 'positive term', a necessary and final meaning, but merely stands in a conventional relation with the signifier. The meaning of a sign is not established by the relation between signifier and signified, but rather between a sign's place within the larger system of signs (la langue). Derrida starts with this point and painstakingly demonstrates what it implies for traditional Western notions of meaning. For Derrida, Saussure's definition of the sign means that meaning can never be contained in the sign. If meaning is relational, every sign having its meaning in terms of its similarity with and difference to other signs, then meaning must itself be relational. When we inquire into the meaning of a sign such as 'culture' we find that its signified turns into a signifier for a series of further signifieds: non-natural, man-made, historical, tasteful, social privilege, superstructure (a Marxist term), language, education are only some of the signifieds which confront us when we attempt to establish the meaning of 'culture'. Each of these new signifieds turns 'culture' into a signifier and yet each of them have meaning only in relation to other signifieds; each of them in turn must become a signifier for a new signified. Meaning, Derrida argues, cannot be pinned down: meaning is, as Saussure had only partially grasped, purely relational. To halt the *play* of meaning (relational movement of signifieds becoming signifiers ad infinitum) we would need to find what Derrida calls a *transcendental signified* (a sign which does not depend upon other signs for its meaning). That there is not and cannot be a transcendental signified (and thus an end to the play of meaning) is the radical lesson of Derrida's deconstructive philosophy. It is a lesson which disrupts (deconstructs) all discourses (philosophical, logical, religious, legalistic, humanistic, scientific) which claim to have direct access to a final and stable meaning and thus truth.

a structure, a language system, then it seems inevitable, only natural, to posit the author as the centre (origin, source) of that structure. Just as God is seen as the author (centre) of the universe as the system or structure in religious discourses, so the literary author is the traditional centre of the work as structure. Indeed, as Derrida remarks, it is difficult to think of any structure (an idea which involves notions of stability and order) without the idea of a centre (point of order, of orientation) (Derrida 1981: 278–9). How can structures be unorganized? They must surely have a point of order, a centre to which all parts of the structure relate.

The apparent necessity of the centre (of the idea of a centred structure) derives from the traditional notion that what we have called, after Derrida, the play of meaning must come to an end, must have an end-point. The centre is that origin or source which allows for the play of meaning and yet which ultimately puts an end to it. The centre is, therefore, not involved in the play of meaning itself and thus not directly involved in the structure produced by that play. Like the author for the literary work, the centre establishes the play of meaning (the structure) but is not involved in that play itself. When we read a literary work we traditionally posit an author behind it, as the originator and the final reference point of the work seen as a structure or system of meanings. As Derrida puts it, teasing out the logical contradictions in such traditional ideas:

> the center . . . closes off the play it opens up and makes possible. As center, it is the point at which the substitution of contents, elements, or terms is no longer possible. . . . Thus it has always been thought that the center, which is by definition unique, constituted that very thing within a structure which while governing the structure, escapes structurality. This is why classical thought concerning structure could say that the center is, paradoxically, *within* the structure and *outside* it. The center is at the center of the totality, and yet, since the center does not belong to the totality (is not part of the totality), the totality *has its center elsewhere*. The center is not the center. The concept of centered structure – although it represents coherence itself, the condition of the *epistēmē* as philosophy or science – is contradictorily coherent.
>
> (1981: 279)

If what we mean by structure is a network of relational meaning – for example, all the ambiguities and tensions and potential combinations which go to make up a literary work – then it seems only natural that we should seek an origin and end-point, a centre, for such meanings. This centre would act as a transcendental signified, in that allowing for the structure itself it would not partake of the structure (play of meanings) but would be its foundation. When we look for such centres, such transcendental signifieds, however, we find that they are, as Derrida puts it, always somewhere else. This means not only that they are always actually outside the structure they apparently stabilize, but also that they themselves have their meaning elsewhere. When we try to posit the author as the centre of a literary work, we find that we cannot stop at that signified. What do we mean by the author? Do we mean that the centre of the work is the author's intention, or his or her emotional needs and desires and anxieties? Is the centre his or her unconscious, or the historical contexts within which he or she wrote? The author, like all apparent transcendental signifieds, turns out to have meaning only as a signifier for other signifieds: aesthetics, psychology, society, history and so on. Derrida writes: 'the entire history of the concept of structure . . . must be thought of as a series of substitutions of center for center, as a linked chain of determinations of the center. Successively, and in a regulated fashion, the center receives different forms or names' (1981: 279). When we ask what the centre of philosophy as a structure is, we are confronted with just such a chain of substitutions: Truth, Knowledge, Logic, Nature, Reality, Being, Right, Divinity, Freedom, History, Language, Science and so on. When we ask for the signified of the signifier God we experience a similar substitutive vertigo: First Cause, Prime Mover, Yahweh, Trinity, Allah, the Tetragrammaton, Spirit, Father, the One, Essence, Knowledge, the Eye that Sees, the Hand that Moves, Love, Vengeance, Forgiveness, the Son, the Mother, the Child, Eternity, Law, the Maker, The Great Architect, Justice and so on.

Structuralism, Derrida suggests, has, like all previous intellectual discourses, erected its method on the basis of a centre, a transcendental signified. This centre, for structuralism, is the idea of the sign itself. As we have seen in the last chapter, Saussure and those who developed his ideas in France and elsewhere, imagined a science of semiology which would be capable of reading all cultural sign systems. Such a method, or general science, relies ultimately on the idea of the sign and its ability to centre (order and scientifically stabilize) such a method. Derrida's deconstructive approach, however, demonstrates that the sign cannot function in this manner. Instead of stable structures (sign systems) which can be definitively analysed by semiologists or structuralists, Derrida presents us with the never-ending play of meaning in language. This play of meaning is given a number of names in Derrida's work and in post-structuralism generally: écriture (writing), différance, textuality. The important point referred to by all these terms, however, is neatly expressed by Derrida: 'The absence of the transcendental signified extends the domain and the play of signification infinitely' (1981: 280). The meaning of signs (signification) cannot be arrested, stopped, finalized, since there is no centre, every signified becoming a new signifier in a process that knows no end.

EMPIRE OF EMPTY SIGNS

We can observe how significantly deconstructive ideas affected Barthes's writing practice by looking at his 1970 study of Japan, *Empire of Signs*. Barthes's purpose in this text is not to produce a semiological study of the signs of Japanese culture, practising the kind of rigorous analysis of first-order and second-order (denotative and connotative) meanings he explores in a text such as *The Fashion System*. Barthes's intention here is to demonstrate how a culture outside of the system of the Western world disturbs and dismantles our preconceptions about how signs work and what meaning is.

What Barthes finds in Japanese culture is a freedom from the Western obsession with meaning: an obsession which can be reduced to the search for meaning within objects, signifieds within signifiers. Barthes knows no Japanese, so the language spoken around him is a pure sound, empty of meaning. Japanese food is served in a totally unhierarchical fashion (no first course, main course, dessert, etc.) and so allows for a pure freedom of combinatory choice for the diner. The Japanese love of packaging fascinates Barthes, as it seems to confirm a culture which is in love with empty signs or signifiers which do not lead to final signifieds. Japanese gifts (even the most trivial) are so elaborately wrapped and packaged that 'It is as if . . . the box were the object of the gift, not what it contains' (ESi: 46). Barthes spends considerable time discussing the tradition of Japanese poetry known as the haiku. J.A. Cuddon defines the haiku in the following way: 'A Japanese verse form consisting of seventeen syllables in three lines of five, seven and five syllables respectively. Such a poem expresses a single idea, image or feeling; in fact, it is a kind of miniature "snap" in words' (Cuddon 1991: 399). The haiku, as a kind of snapshot of time or feeling, seems to present a perfect emblem for Barthes's own approach in *Empire of Signs*.

Presenting apparently disconnected descriptions of and meditations on diverse aspects of Japanese culture, Barthes's text does not build up to an ultimate and final analysis or overarching meaning. Such an approach would be completely opposed to Barthes's intention here since, as he says, his desire is not to capture the reality of Japanese culture (whatever that may be) but rather to respond as a visitor who is desirous to escape the Western itch for meaning. Japan, then, provides limitless opportunities for a release from meaning, for a pleasurable floating among empty languages, empty signs. The haiku poem is mere surface, has no hidden or ultimate signified (no centre, in Derrida's sense) and thus is a kind of pure writing. This is precisely the status and effect Barthes aims for in his own writing in *Empire of Signs*.

Derrida's deconstruction of the Western reliance on notions of the transcendental signified and of centred structure could be said, despite its hugely radical and innovatory implications for all branches of the 'human sciences', to confirm at least one tendency of Barthes's earlier work. In works such as *Writing Degree Zero*, *Mythologies* and *The Fashion System*, as we have observed, Barthes attacks bourgeois society's tendency to give a covering of meaning to everything. Barthes, from the outset of his career, has attacked the process whereby artificial objects, mass-produced images, processes of power or social manipulation are solidified into apparently natural signs. *Empire of Signs* is a deconstructive fiction of a space (here called Japan) freed from the Western anxiety and obsession with clear, stable, singular meaning. The text is an antidote to the Western sign (always full, always attached to a definite signified). Thus Barthes describes Tokyo, one of the most populated cities in the world, as a site which, unlike Western cities, has its centre to one side. The Emperor's residence is a decentred and thus empty centre as read by Barthes:

> The entire city turns around a site both forbidden and indifferent, a residence concealed beneath foliage, protected by moats, inhabited by an emperor who is never seen, which is to say, literally, by no one knows who. Daily, in their rapid, energetic, bullet-like trajectories, the taxis avoid this circle, whose low crest, the visible form of invisibility, hides the sacred 'nothing.'
>
> (ESi: 30–2)

Similarly, Tokyo streets have no names, the inhabitants and visitors orienting themselves through the use of visual, hand-written guides and by visual memory. Barthes comments: 'to visit a place for the first time is thereby to begin to write it: the address not being written, it must establish its own writing' (ESi: 36).

This idea of writing Japan, of being provoked (by an absence of meaning) into an act of writing, is crucial and takes us to the heart of this particular text's importance for Barthes's post-structuralist phase of work. Barthes does not go out to produce a cultural analysis of Japan. As Barthes recognizes at the very beginning of his text, such a procedure would merely repeat the myth of the Orient, from which no Westerner is exempt. Instead of such a Western diagnosis of the Orient, Barthes reads Japan as a text. More importantly, he reads Japan as a text which remains, ultimately, unreadable, beyond the recuperation (discovery) of the kind of stable and finite meaning for which reading traditionally seeks. As Barthes puts it in a 1970 interview: 'in Japan, as I read things, there is no supreme signified to anchor the chain of signs, there is no keystone;' this, he adds, 'permits signs to flourish with great subtlety and freedom' (GV: 99). Japan, as a text whose signs are not 'anchored' in a 'supreme signified' (a centre or transcendental signified), provokes Barthes into a form of writing. The reader, faced with signifiers which are not anchored in one ultimate signified, must become a writer, someone who re-creates the text, who draws his or her own temporary structures and patterns and meanings upon that text. It is this process, in which reading becomes writing, which most significantly characterizes Barthes's post-structuralist theories of the text, the author and the reader.

THE DEATH OF THE AUTHOR

Barthes's 1968 essay 'The Death of the Author' is perhaps the most widely read essay he ever wrote. Studied in countless university courses and cited in thousands of academic articles, it has led to a cultural myth of Barthes himself. To cite just one recent publisher's statement or blurb: 'Roland Barthes was a leading expert in semiology and cultural theory; he became notorious for his announcement of "The Death of the Author" in 1968.' We have already seen that rather more pressing events were occurring in 1968 than Barthes's brief articulation of post-structuralist theory, and it is clearly part of the mythologizing process of such pronouncements to help create the notoriety to which they seem innocently to refer. 'The Death of the Author', is, however, a usefully condensed expression of Barthes's developing post-structuralist approach to the issues of reading, writing, and the relationship between texts and the signs which comprise them.

The author, Barthes notes, has always functioned within capitalist society as the 'anchor' of the literary work's signifiers. The author is posited as the centre of the work: the origin of all the work's meaning, the author is also that figure towards which all reading should direct itself. Barthes writes: '*explanation* of the work is still sought in the person of its producer, as if, through the more or less transparent allegory of fiction, it was always, ultimately, the voice of one and the same person, the *author*, which was transmitting his "confidences"' (RL: 50).

Such an idea of the author involves us in the traditional system of meaning which is the object of Derrida's deconstructive critique. The author, traditionally, is a transcendental signified, standing behind the work as God is thought to stand behind the material universe. A divine figure, in this sense, the author thus gives stability and order to the work. Barthes's essay, in fact, lays bare the figurative associations made in Western male-dominated society between God, the father, and the author. As he puts it: 'the Author is supposed to *feed* the book, i.e., he lives before it, thinks, suffers, lives for it; he has the same relation of antecedence with his work that a father sustains with his child' (RL: 52). This filial myth of the author is a particularly convenient one for capitalist or commercialized ideas of reading, since it allows for a model in which works can be deciphered, successfully interpreted, fully understood and thus tamed. The figure of the author, that is, is designed to reduce the play of meaning, to bring it to an end, in fact. In a thematically related essay of the same year, 'What is an Author?', Michel Foucault had argued that 'The author is . . . the ideological figure by which one marks the manner in which we fear the proliferation of meaning' (Foucault 1979: 159). Barthes's critique of the figure of the author is similarly oriented towards the manner in which that figure contains, limits and ultimately tames meaning (RL: 53).

Barthes's essay can be said to be a transitional one, in that within it the movement from structuralism to post-structuralism can be detected. It needs to be noted that it is not the idea of the 'death of the author' which makes such an essay post-structuralist. With its focus on system rather than the traditional notion of work-and-author as site of meaning, structuralism had already dispensed with the figure of the author. What makes this essay post-structuralist is the emergence within it of the theory of the text and of intertextuality and, in particular, of ideas associated with the radical theoretical journal *Tel Quel*.

In 'The Death of the Author' Barthes expresses ideas close to the heart of the journal *Tel Quel*: he argues that to use the figure of the author to stabilize meaning is to join modern, Western society's attempt to present itself in possession of a singular, unified and indisputable meaning or Truth. The radical celebration of plurality and the infinite play of meaning within literary and other kinds of work had, by 1968, become associated with a number of key terms in *Tel Quel* theory in particular and post-structuralist work in general. The most

TEL QUEL

Tel Quel is the title of an influential theoretical journal published between 1960 and 1983, after which time it was renamed *L'Infini*. The journal takes its name from the title of a work by the influential French writer Paul Valéry (1871–1945), and it began with a concern to celebrate literature *tel quel* 'such as it is'. By the period between 1966 and 1975 the journal had grown into the most significant forum for work pushing theory beyond its structuralist and into its post-structuralist phase (see ffrench 1995 and 1998). Edited by a committee, but particularly associated in its major period with Philippe Sollers, *Tel Quel* published many groundbreaking articles by Derrida, Kristeva, Foucault, Louis Althusser (1918–90) and Barthes himself, and popularized the work of important writers such as Georges Bataille (1897–1962). Always concerned to promote the most radical forms of new writing and theory, *Tel Quel* by 1968 had developed a primary concern with the plurality of language, especially literary language. Associated with support for the radical left-wing politics of the period, *Tel Quel* theory, expressed in works by Kristeva, Barthes, Derrida and others, pitted radical (plural) notions of language and writing against modern, capitalist values of consumption and stable meaning.

important of these terms for Barthes's own development are *writing*, *text*, and various ideas and terms concerning the linguistic and psychological *subject*. Writing, in an essay such as 'The Death of the Author', begins to be a term which refers to language that does not posit or depend upon an ultimate signified. We might say that Japan itself, the strange text of Japan that Barthes confronts and partly constructs, is a realm of writing in this sense. A new sense of literature's potential for critique of and freedom from dominant cultural ideology begins to emerge here and is registered in many of Barthes's comments in his essay. As he writes:

> literature (it would be better, from now on, to say *writing*), by refusing to assign to the text (and to the world-as-text) a 'secret,' i.e., an ultimate meaning, liberates an activity we may call countertheological, properly revolutionary, for to refuse to halt meaning is finally to refuse God and his hypostases, reason, science, the law.

(RL: 54)

To posit an author as centre of a literary work is to join with capitalist society in suppressing difference (the proliferation of meaning in language). To work to unleash writing (language in its radical plurality) is to partake in an act that in Barthes's terms is clearly at once linguistically and politically radical. *Tel Quel* theory associates notions of clear and stable meaning with consumerism and consumption: society, argues Barthes and Kristeva, wants us to believe that there is a consumable (clear, decipherable, readable, finite) meaning in all texts. Literature, in this sense, is treated by dominant society as a branch of consumerism: the reader being encouraged to buy books, read them, find their meaning, thus exhaust them, and then buy another book. The connection between literary books, chocolate bars, soap-powders, compact discs and items of clothing should be obvious. *Tel Quel* theory seeks to resist the absorption of literature into a culture of mass-produced and consumed products. Writing, when freed from its fictional basis in the author, works to disrupt notions of consumption:

> In multiple writing, in effect, everything is to be *disentangled*, but nothing *deciphered*, structure can be followed, 'threaded' (as we say of a run in a stocking) in all its reprises, all its stages, but there is no end to it, no bottom; the space of writing is to be traversed, not pierced; writing constantly posits meaning, but always in order to evaporate it: writing seeks a systematic exemption of meaning.
>
> (RL: 53–4)

Where does such a writing, free from the confines of the author, exempt from any final signified, exist? The answer for Barthes is in the notion of *the text*, which is clearly distinguished from the more traditional notion of a work with an author behind it. As Barthes famously states:

> We know now that a text consists not of a line of words, releasing a single 'theological' meaning (the 'message' of the Author-God), but of a multidimensional space in which are married and contested several writings, none of which is original: the text is a fabric of quotations, resulting from a thousand sources of culture.
>
> (RL: 52–3)

Behind Barthes's argument concerning the death of the author lies a developing theory of what he here calls the text.

SUMMARY

Barthes's post-structuralist phase is characterized by a movement away from the idea of a scientific and objective methodology. Semiotics and structuralism, as practised by Barthes in works such as *The Fashion System* and 'Introduction to the Structural Analysis of Narratives', are now viewed as dependent on a questionable idea of the sign. We began this chapter by looking at how Barthes begins to produce a radical critique of the sign itself. Barthes is influenced in this by theorists such as Jacques Derrida, and it is through such influences that Barthes's work begins to explore the radical force of the signifier, rather than the sign (with its assumption of stable signifieds for signifiers). The signifier, which does not lead to final signifieds, presents us with a space (city, culture) characterized by the empty sign in *Empire of Signs*; it also begins to contribute to a wholesale critique of the traditional notion of the author and thus to a radically new sense of the relationship between reader, text and meaning.

6

TEXTUALITY

In this chapter we will continue with our look at Barthes's post-structuralist work, focusing now in particular on the theory of the text and intertextuality. Barthes's *S/Z*, first published in 1970, is a hugely important work not only in this phase of his career but in his career in general. It is in *S/Z* that Barthes's theory of the text is fully articulated and, as a consequence, it is in this seminal work that the move from the structuralist analysis of narratives to a post-structuralist approach to narratives, and indeed to literary language in general, can be fully appreciated.

THEORY OF THE TEXT

The attack on the sign which we have observed in the work of Barthes and Derrida involves concerns other than those relating to the instability of the signified (its tendency to become another signifier). Kristeva's introduction, in the late 1960s, of the work of the Russian socio-linguist, Mikhail Bakhtin (1895–1975), is a major source of what we are calling the theory of the text. Bakhtin's work, since Kristeva first introduced it to a European audience, has had an immense impact on linguistics, literary theory and criticism, philosophy, sociology and many other disciplines. His most crucial insight, and the one most thoroughly explored in Kristeva's work, concerns the *dialogic* nature of language.

DIALOGISM

Bakhtin, in works such as *Marxism and the Philosophy of Language*, argues against Saussure's focus on language as a system (la langue). Saussure's decision not to focus on actual speech (parole) is a fundamental error, according to Bakhtin, since for him language always and only exists in social situations between actual speakers. Saussure's approach is 'abstract' and spuriously 'objective', according to Bakhtin, and it must be corrected by moving to the actual speech to be found in the numerous social contexts within which language is used. When we do look at language in this way, Bakhtin argues, we find various important phenomena. Language is always *evaluative*, always involved in social ideology. There is no innocent, neutral or objective language, a point which can be grasped by imagining a simple word, such as 'friend', used in different social situations: a bar, a classroom, a job interview, a religious service, a television interview, a novel or a philosophical treatise. The word 'friend', like all words, has different meanings in different situations. The only site in which such a word would be neutral, beyond ideology, would be in a dictionary, but dictionaries, as Bakhtin argues, are not where language as a social phenomenon exists. Language is dialogic, it is always involved in the relations between specific speakers in specific social situations. This feature of language alerts us to the fact that no language user creates meaning independently. The specific social situations in which we use language are associated with different *speech genres* (Bakhtin 1986). We use different languages or discourses (different codes of address, different words and registers) when speaking to someone in an interview, in our own home, in a classroom, in a church, at a football match or a funeral service. Our dialogue as speakers, therefore, is not simply with those we speak with but also with the already established codes and modes of speaking associated with different social situations. Our words are never simply our own but are dialogic, possessing within them what has already been said before us. There is an 'otherness' in all our words, therefore: the 'otherness' of what has already been said. Bakhtin refers to 'double-voiced discourse', to the manner in which our words (spoken or written) always have more than one meaning, one 'voice' within them (see Bakhtin 1984). This fact, for Bakhtin, is not a matter of regret but testifies to the positive social nature (the dialogic nature) of all language; a feature of language (Bakhtin sometimes refers to *heteroglossia* or 'multivoiced' language) which dominant society frequently attempts to repress in favour of the idea of one voice, one meaning, one Truth (*monoglossia*). In Bakhtin's work the dialogic force in language and society is promoted and celebrated in contrast to the monologic tendency of dominant ideology and power (for further discussion of Bakhtin and of Kristeva's reworking of his ideas, see Allen 2000: 8–60).

Kristeva's influential readings of Bakhtin (see Kristeva 1980: 36–63 and 64–91) find within his work the basis for a model of literary (Kristeva uses the term 'poetic') language in which language is always double, always involved in polysemy (multiple meaning). Famously, Kristeva takes Bakhtin's dialogic account of language and generates out of it a new theory of literary language in terms of *intertextuality*. We can register the direct influence of this key idea on Barthes in the quotation with which we concluded the last section of Chapter 5.

Intertextuality is a crucial concept within Barthes's developing theory of the text. It is the idea, above any other, that allows Barthes to begin a description of the literary text outside of the traditional confines of authorship. The author, after all, is merely the compiler of intertextual meaning and relations:

> the writer can only imitate an ever anterior, never original gesture; his sole power is to mingle writings, to counter some by others, so as never to rely on just one; if he seeks to *express himself*, at least he knows that the interior 'thing' he claims to 'translate' is itself no more than a ready-made lexicon, whose words can be explained only through other words, and this ad infinitum . . .
>
> (RL: 53)

The theory of intertextuality destroys traditional notions of the origin of meaning, whether they are located in the sign (with a presumed stable signified) or the author (presumed God-like creator of meaning). There can be no origin of the meaning of a literary text since its intertextual nature means that it is always comprised of pre-existing textual elements, a 'tissue of quotations'. The author is no longer, in this theory, the originator of meaning, since meaning no longer has an origin.

INTERTEXTUALITY

Intertextuality has become a major term in literary studies and has been given various definitions by leading theorists and critics (see Allen 2000; for Barthes and intertextuality, see 61–94). In Kristeva, intertextuality is a term referring to the dialogic nature of literary language. The literary text is no longer viewed as a unique and autonomous entity but as the product of a host of pre-existent codes, discourses and previous texts. Every word in a text in this sense is intertextual and so must be read not only in terms of a meaning presumed to exist within the text itself, but also in terms of meaningful relations stretching far outside the text into a host of cultural discourses. Intertextuality, in this sense, questions our apparently common-sensical notions of what is *inside* and what *outside* the text, viewing meaning as something that can never be contained and constrained within the text itself. There is a mistaken tendency in readers of Kristeva to confuse intertextuality with more traditional, author-based concepts, particularly the concept of *influence*. Intertextuality is not, however, an intended reference by an author to another text: intertextuality is the very condition of signification, of meaning, in literary and indeed all language.

It should be noted here that the death of the author is not a phenomenon which begins with post-structuralism. Our analysis of the structural analysis of narratives in Chapter 4 demonstrates that structuralism itself finds no place for the author as the originator of meaning. In structuralism a text's meaning stems not from the author but from the system out of which the text is produced. The post-structuralist theory of the text does not kill the author, since this has already occurred in structuralism itself. The theory of the text, as articulated by Barthes, does not so much announce the death of the author as the death of the reader as envisioned within structuralism. It is structuralism's idea of the reader operating at an objective and exhaustive level, possessing a scientific (linguistic) model of language and therefore of literary texts, which is challenged and ultimately destroyed by the post-structuralist theory of the text.

Barthes famously states, in his essay on that topic, that 'the birth of the reader must be requited by the death of the Author' (RL: 55). But this is a new reader, a reader of the text. As Barthes explains in related essays, such as 'From Work to Text' (RL: 56–64) and 'Theory of the

Text', the reader of the text is not confronted with a stable, self-contained object but rather with a 'methodological field' (RL: 57). Contrasting the traditional author-based notion of *the work* with *the text*, Barthes states that while a work can be held in the hand and seen on the shelves of libraries and bookshops, the text only exists when it is produced by the new reader: '*the Text is experienced only in an activity, in a production*' (RL: 58). Text is an ancient word, as Barthes reminds us, involving notions of spinning and weaving: it is the word from which we derive our word for manufactured cloth or textiles. The text is a woven or spun phenomenon in that it is made up of 'quotations, references, echoes' (RL: 60). And yet this intertextual weave is potentially infinite: we are not dealing with sources and origins when we come to the text but rather with the *already written* and the *already said*: 'the quotations a text is made of are anonymous, irrecoverable, and yet *already read*: they are quotations without quotations marks' (RL: 60). To read a modern love poem as a work will almost inevitably involve tracing the author's ideas and feelings from apparent signs in that work. The author's love life will be taken as the signified of the poem's signifiers. To read the same poem as a text, however, involves us in the vast array of codes and conventions, genres and discourses, which make up the modern and the traditional notions of love and love poetry in our society. This text's signifiers come from and direct our attention towards the vast field of cultural discourses on love, hardly something that can function as a signified. Such a text certainly has meaning; in fact, it has an overwhelming amount of potential meaning. It is not, however, fully a text, not fully something that signifies, until the reader has set going (opened) its intertextual threads and provided a limited structure or what Barthes calls *structuration*. Structure, a concept which in structuralism relates to the system (la langue) out of which texts (parole) are generated is now, in Barthes's theory of the text, something provided by the reader. The reader produces the text's structure: as Barthes states: 'the unity of a text is not in its origin but in its destination' (RL: 54).

TEXTUAL ANALYSIS

In his 'Theory of the Text' Barthes takes a term previously employed by Kristeva which encapsulates the nature of meaning in the text. If the term signification relates to the received notion of the sign (signifiers leading to stable signifieds), then *signifiance* refers to a meaning which must be produced by the reader. Signification is the concern of all those interpretive approaches to the text which seek a final signified behind its signifiers. We have looked at the search for an author as signified, but Barthes here reminds us that there are other approaches which seek a centre, origin and thus final signified behind or below the text: Marxist criticism, for example, seeks a socio-historical signified as origin of all texts (TT: 37). In such approaches, Barthes writes: 'the text is treated as if it were the repository of an objective signification, and this signification appears as embalmed in the work-as-product'. However, as Barthes adds:

> once the text is conceived as production (and no longer as product), 'signifi-
> cation' is no longer an adequate concept. As soon as the text is conceived as
> a polysemic space where the paths of several possible meanings intersect, it
> is necessary to cast off the monological, legal status of signification, and to
> pluralise it.
>
> (TT: 37)

Barthes uses signifiance to refer to the text as something *in production*, something produced as much by the reader as by the language of the text itself (TT: 37–8).

In a number of essays of this period Barthes sketches out what he calls *textual analysis* and the manner in which such an activity calls for a *production* of the text, an analysis of signifiance rather than signification. These essays, collected in *The Semiotic Challenge*, mark the distinction between the structural analysis of narratives and textual analysis. The former seeks to establish how a text is constructed; the latter seeks to trace the text's 'avenues of meaning', to explore the manner in which meaning 'explodes and scatters' (SC: 262). Barthes's greatest example of textual analysis, and his most exhaustive account of the theory of the text, however, comes in his *S/Z*, an analysis of a short story by Balzac entitled *Sarrasine*.

In 1970, the year Barthes published *S/Z*, *Sarrasine* was a relatively underdiscussed text in Balzac's canon of work. Part of Balzac's *Scènes de la Vie Parisienne* (*Tales of Parisian Life*), *Sarrasine* is a disturbing twenty-page story existing somewhere between Gothic intrigue, comic tale of ignorance and psychological study of the illusions of love. The fashion-able Lanty family have a secret: what is or was the source of their considerable wealth? A young female party-goer engages the narrator, another guest at the party at the Lanty dwelling, and enquires about a mysterious old man who forms some kind of relation to the beautiful younger members of the household. An exquisite painting of Adonis 'copied from the statue of a woman' (S/Z: 232) adds to the accumulating mysteries since there seems to be some connection between this painting, the original statue and the old man, object of the young woman's curiosity. A deal is struck between the young woman and the narrator: the narrator will reveal the mystery if the young woman will respond positively to the narrator's desire for her.

The mystery involves a sculptor called Sarrasine who goes to Rome at a young age. At the opera he falls in love with a beautiful singer named La Zambinella. Attending the opera every night Sarrasine eventually meets with his beloved whom he has used as the model for an incredibly idealized statue. La Zambinella is at once encouraging and discouraging to Sarrasine, teetering between vivacity and immense melancholy. Sarrasine, in desperation at such mixed signals, decides to kidnap the object of all his emotional and aesthetic desires. He hatches a plan to abduct La Zambinella after she has performed at a private function at the French ambassador's residence. In attendance at this function is La Zambinella's chief admirer and sponsor, Cardinal Cicognara. La Zambinella is in the middle of the performance when Sarrasine enters. His beloved is 'dressed like a man . . . wearing a snood, kinky hair, and a sword' (S/Z: 250). Previously, Zambinella had asked of Sarrasine what he would do if he discovered that she was not a woman. Yet Sarrasine's passion had proved far too strong to entertain such ridiculous ideas. Sarrasine, even after having entered the ambassador's residence, remains confident of his judgement: he is, after all, an artist, and artists know about beauty. Sarrasine cannot avoid reality forever, however: Zambinella is a castrato, as indeed are all the 'female' characters on the Roman stage, since the law forbids female performers. Everybody in Rome knows this, it is a commonplace. Sarrasine in a rage proceeds with his abduction of Zambinella, still in love but now capable of murder. It is Sarrasine, however, who is eventually murdered by assassins hired by Cardinal Cicognara.

The old man at the Lanty's party is Zambinella in old age. His wealth, gained as a star on the Italian operatic scene, is the source of the Lanty family's wealth. The old man was, in youth, the model for the statue upon which the painting of Adonis was based. At the heart or centre of the mystery which the young woman asked the narrator to unveil lies an emptiness, a nothingness, a tale of castration. Castration, a phenomenon which replaces the patriarchal sign of fullness (the phallus) with an absence, an emptiness, appals the young woman and the implicit contract between her and the narrator is broken. She decides, in horror, that the world has no meaning and leaves the narrator unfulfilled and 'pensive'.

Barthes's textual analysis of this intriguing short story lasts for over two hundred pages. It consists of a painstaking piece-by-piece structuration of the story, interspersed with compelling theoretical meditations on narrative, realism, literature, textuality, language and other characteristic Barthesian themes. Barthes's structuration is based on a method of cutting the text up into small units of meaning, or lexias. A lexia, Barthes writes, is an arbitrary unit of reading rather than a necessary one. Other readers will inevitably discover alternative lexias. Lexias are simply units in which the reader who is actively producing the text discovers the *explosion* and *scattering* of meaning. They are units of reading in which a group of connotations are discovered within the signifier (S/Z: 13–14). Barthes refers figuratively to 'the starred text', the lexias functioning as stars that break up the narrative. Thus, Zambinella as a name is a lexia; a very significant one, in fact, since the alternation in the text between the feminine La Zambinella (with 'La') and the masculine Zambinella (without 'La') plays a crucial role in the disguises and blind-spots which fuel much of the drama. Likewise, Sarrasine's name, with its feminine ending (e), is another lexia. Eventually, as the title of Barthes's study demonstrates, the strange mirror relationship between S and Z will come to possess great symbolic resonances.

What the lexias ultimately allow for is the emergence of various codes. Barthes employs five codes in his attempt to capture something of how meaning is produced and dispersed in the text. Two of these codes have to do with the manner in which the narrative produces itself, that is to say, they have to do with narrative and chronological logic. The *hermeneutic code* (HER) concerns all those units:

> whose function it is to articulate in various ways a question, its response, and the variety of chance events which can either formulate the question or delay its answer; or even, constitute an enigma and lead to its solution.

(S/Z: 17)

The question concerning the source of the Lanty family's wealth, for example, is a major example of the hermeneutic code. The code of actions or the *proairetic code* (ACT) corresponds in many respects to the level of 'Actions' discussed previously in Barthes's essay on the structural analysis of narratives: it is a code concerned with actions and their effects: 'each effect' having 'a generic name giving a kind of title to the sequence' (S/Z: 18). Thus, for example, as our plot summary above suggests, there are certain sequences (such as 'Courtship', 'Abduction', 'Assassination') observable in the text.

The three remaining codes have for their reference chains of meaning which take us outside of the text's narrative sequences and logic. The *symbolic code* (SYM) concerns all the symbolic patterns, particularly the patterns of antithesis and opposition, observable in the text. There are, for example, huge areas of Balzac's text concerned with symbolic antithesis between the sexes. The *code of semes* (SEM) concerns all the connotations which build up the qualities of characters or actions. A typical seme for La Zambinella is, of course, 'Femininity'. The *cultural code* (REF) concerns 'the numerous codes of knowledge or wisdom to which the text continually refers'. Barthes notes that, while 'all codes' are in a sense 'cultural', what he is calling cultural codes here 'afford the discourse a basis in scientific or moral authority' and are thus also nameable as 'reference codes' (S/Z: 18). A recurrent set of cultural codes in this story concerns, for example, the received literary and moral codes concerning love and passion.

Like the 561 lexias Barthes locates and discusses, the five codes are not simply *there* in the text. They are convenient tools which Barthes brings to the text in his active, productive structuration of the text. They are tools designed by Barthes to register the 'difference' of the text, by which he means not its uniqueness (the text, as he rigorously shows, is woven from the intertextual, from the *already written* and *already read*) but its plurality, the unfinished and unfinishable nature of its significance. The two narrative (sequential) codes (hermeneutic and proairetic), however, work to close off this plurality of meaning, seeking to produce a chronological movement from beginning to end in which a mystery (enigma) is ultimately solved. The other three codes (we might call them, collectively, the non-sequential codes) work against the narrative codes, producing meanings which disrupt the narrative flow and development, taking the reader and indeed the text into intertextual fields outside of the story. In this sense, the two narrative codes seek to make the text irreversible (a narrative working on a linear or syntagmatic dimension). The three non-sequential codes produce a reversibility in the text, allowing us to break the narrative or syntagmatic order of sequences and experience the text's explosion and dispersal into the intertextual, into the cultural text. *Sarrasine* is, then, a text which Barthes describes as possessing a limited plurality, against which he contrasts modern, avant-garde texts which are completely reversible, entirely pluralized.

WRITERLY AND READERLY TEXTS

Barthes's opposition between irreversible and reversible textual elements allows him to build up a theory concerning the *lisible* (readerly) text and *scriptible* (writerly) text. There is often a tendency in commentary on Barthes's work to see this opposition in a straightforwardly historical manner: classical, pre-modern texts being readerly and thus irreversible; modern, avant-garde texts being writerly and thus entirely reversible. In his essay 'From Work to Text', however, Barthes makes it clear that 'there can be "Text" in a very old work, and many products of contemporary literature are not texts at all' (RL: 57). The opposition, in fact, has more to do with Barthes's attack on the commodification of literature and the socially sanctioned association between what is consumable and what is clearly communicated. As Barthes puts it: 'Why is the writerly our value? Because the goal of literary work (of literature as work) is to make the reader no longer a consumer, but a producer of the text' (RL: 4). A purely readerly text, irreversible in all its features, leaves the reader with no productive work: 'instead of gaining access to the magic of the signifier, to the pleasure of writing, he is left no more than the poor freedom either to accept or to reject the text' (ibid.).

Balzac's *Sarrasine*, as we have noted, is a partially reversible text: it has a degree of 'Text' or textuality within it. It is a large part of the work of Barthes in *S/Z* to show how such an apparently classical text can be written by the reader. The conflict between what I have called the sequential and non-sequential codes describes precisely the possibilities and the limits of such a writing on the part of the reader. In fact, the brilliance of Barthes's reading is to demonstrate, in quite unexpected ways, the manner in which Balzac's text establishes a metatextual commentary on this very issue. Sarrasine, after all, is eventually killed by his too passive acceptance of the signifiers which surround him. Ignorant of the cultural connotations of Italian operatic performances, he is equally a slave to cultural clichés concerning art, beauty and femininity. Sarrasine is the victim of what Barthes calls false logic or *endoxal* thinking: the *doxa* is common sense, public opinion, cliché, dominant ideology, the idea of stable and singular signifieds behind signifiers. Myths, as read by Barthes, involve endoxal thinking, in that they present certain signifieds as inevitable, natural and unchallengeable. In one episode Zambinella is frightened by a snake; Sarrasine kills the snake and interprets Zambinella's fright as proof positive of her womanhood. Endoxal logic, after all, would have us believe that behind signs of temerity lies a stable signified: femininity. Sarrasine is full of such false proofs and Barthes uses the ancient rhetorical term of the *enthymeme* to describe them. An enthymeme is a syllogism (a logical proof: *all men are mortal; Socrates is a man; thus Socrates is mortal*) but with a piece or step missing. Thus, as Barthes writes, Sarrasine is constantly snaring himself into false proofs by too quickly reaching for the obvious (in the sense of culturally commonplace) signified (S/Z: 167). Sarrasine, in fact, Barthes writes, acts like the reader of a realist novel who takes the artificial codes that generate the illusion of realism for reality itself. *S/Z*, along with everything else it is, is a further chapter in Barthes's life-long critique of realism. As he puts it:

> the 'realistic' artist never places 'reality' at the origin of his discourse, but only and always, as far back as can be traced, an already written real, a prospective code, along which we discern, as far as the eye can see, only a succession of copies.
>
> (S/Z: 167)

Sarrasine is a fictional character who thinks he exists in a realist world, which is to say he believes that the world around him is readable on a realist basis (signifiers having obvious and determinate signifieds). He is ignorant of the fact that the world around him, and indeed his own character, is part of a cultural writing, a world of pre-existent codes. He is rather like a visitor to Japan, the Empire of Empty Signs, who assumes that all signifiers have stable and clear signifieds and so reads every sign he encounters in this way, filling them with his own naïve semiotic preconceptions.

Balzac's text is thus partially lisible and partially scriptible; it allows Barthes to indulge in a limited rewriting. The idea of a completely plural text, wholly reversible, and thus demanding a complete productivity, a complete writing on the part of the reader, would seem to be Barthes's post-structuralist version of the zero-degree writing he championed in his first book, or the 'objective' writing he temporarily found in the novels of Robbe-Grillet. Such a purely scriptible text would escape endoxal logic in that it would offer no possibility of moving out of the realm of the signifier towards the closed realm of final signifieds. Barthes gives the following description of such a text:

> the networks are many and interact, without any one of them being able to surpass the rest; this text is a galaxy of signifiers, not a structure of signifieds; it has no beginning; it is reversible; we gain access to it by several entrances, none of which can be authoritatively declared to be the main one; the codes it mobilizes extend *as far as the eye can reach*, they are indeterminable.
>
> (SW: 5–6)

The italicized phrase alludes to work by Barthes's colleague in the *Tel Quel* group, Philippe Sollers (see Sollers 1986: 1). Sollers's novel *Drame* is the subject of an important essay by Barthes in which it is presented in terms of the writerly ideal (SW: 39–67 and Sollers 1986: 85–104). Many aspects of Sollers's text qualify it as a radically scriptible text: it presents no story and is thus entirely free from the narrative (irreversible) codes. It escapes the illusions of realism by recognizing that every object in the world is already signified, already part of the intertextual. The world represented in *Drame*, then, is not one of objects to be read but rather a realm of writing (or intertextuality) within which objects (always already signified) stand on the same level as language (SW: 59). Behind the world of *Drame* stands not an inferred reality (as in realistic modes of fiction) but merely further words, further levels of writing.

The most important feature, and the one which seems most clearly to qualify Sollers's *Drame* as a plural, completely reversible text, concerns what happens in this text to the traditional grammatical markers of speech. We can understand this feature of Sollers's writing by returning to Barthes's reading of Balzac and to the various moments in which Barthes registers a disturbance in the traditional relations between narrative utterance (the narrative 'I') and the apparent thoughts of the story's characters. In one example, used again to open his text on 'The Death of the Author', Barthes takes as a lexia the sentence: 'This was woman herself, with her sudden fears, her irrational whims, her instinctive worries, her impetuous boldness, her fussings, and her delicious sensibility' (S/Z: 172). The sentence occurs immediately after the episode in which Zambinella has been frightened by the appearance of a snake. Barthes asks the question 'Who is speaking?'. It cannot be the narrator, since he knows that Zambinella is a castrated man. It cannot be Sarrasine, since he is not the narrator. If it is Balzac, then why is he indulging in the fiction that Zambinella is a woman? And why is he here suddenly replacing his own voice for the voice of the narrator? Barthes asks: 'Who is speaking? Is it Sarrasine? the narrator? the author? Balzac-the-author? Balzac-the-man? romanticism? bourgeoisie? universal wisdom? The intersecting of all these origins creates the writing' (S/Z: 172–3).

In such moments the traditional conventions of narration are shattered. Conventional narratives employ a narrative voice (the voice of the narrator), although as readers we often infer within that voice the thoughts and beliefs and messages of the author. We may sometimes infer the voice of the author within the utterances of characters; however, it is crucial for traditional approaches to narrative fiction (and indeed all literature) to keep an ultimate separation between narrative voice, the utterances of characters and the inferred message (voice) of the author. In Barthes's example a disturbance is created in this order or hierarchy of voices: a disturbing process since it suggests that there is no longer an ability to separate the voices of the text from the voice of the author behind the text. Such a moment opens up the possibility that what is writing the text is not an ultimate, speaking subject (the author) but the general codes and conventions and intertextual discourses which make up the cultural text. Such a cultural text exists prior to, and forms the foundation for, the text in question; but it also exists prior to the author and creates him or her as a thinking, writing subject.

The possibility opened up in Barthes's example is that it is writing itself (the vast, intertextual realm of the cultural text) which produces the sentence examined here. Such a possibility positions author and text on the same plane: the plane of writing. The author's voice is simply that, another voice; every voice constitutes a part of the *already written*, the *already said*, the *already read*. Sollers's text, Barthes argues, recognizes and utilizes this radical challenge to conventional notions of meaning and the human subject's relation to language. It is a text in which the established modes of speaking are put in question. In *Drame* the narrator is simply part of the story and the basic pronouns by which we mark the 'subject of speech' ('I' and 'he') are alternated, like the black-and-white pieces on a chessboard (SW: 48). The voice that narrates Sollers's *Drame*, in other words, does not lead us back to an authorial voice outside of and existing prior to the text. Sollers's narrative voice is simply part of the text and as such shatters the traditional methods of reading whereby we infer an authorial subject as the signified of the text's signifying voices.

The radically scriptible text, therefore, does more than simply involve the reader in writing (activating, producing) it as text. More profoundly, it questions very fundamental notions of language's relation to the human subject and of what it is to be a human subject. Such texts suggest that, as subjects, we are ourselves part of textuality or writing, the products of the vast codes, conventions and discourses which make up the cultural text within which we think and write. The search for an author behind the text leads, ultimately, only to further writing, further textuality; and yet we, as readers, are also part of that vast intertextual arena. Barthes's final phase of work in the 1970s is greatly concerned with what post-structuralist approaches to language, the sign and textuality do to our conventional notions of the subject in language.

SUMMARY

In this chapter we have seen how Barthes develops a theory of the text in which intertextuality disrupts established ideas concerning meaning, the author, the reader and ultimately the human subject itself. Barthes's textual analysis is, unlike structuralist approaches, unscientific, provisional and exists as an unrepeatable production. Contrasting the readerly with the writerly text, Barthes emphasizes the fact that the latter calls for a productive writing of the text on the part of the reader. The critique of the sign culminates here in a celebration of signifiance, a mode of meaning which does not offer a final, stable signified, but which is in process and thus remains within the realm of the signifier. Following such theoretical moves within Barthes's post-structuralist work has allowed us to trace the connections between his textual analysis of Balzac in *S/Z* and his championing of the contemporary fiction of Philippe Sollers.

7

NEUTRAL WRITING

Pleasure, violence and the novelistic

Barthes's writing in the 1970s increasingly resists the tendency in language to revert to the signified (stable meaning) and thus to undermine or simply absorb writing (language on the level of the signifier). Acutely aware of the violent potential within language, Barthes in works such as *The Pleasure of the Text* (1973), *Roland Barthes by Roland Barthes* (1975) and *A Lover's Discourse: Fragments* (1977) developed theoretical approaches to writing texts which move ever further away from anything that might be described as generalized, methodological or even repeatable.

DOXA AND PARA-DOXA

Roland Barthes by Roland Barthes is a text which provides us with a host of stunning insights into Barthes's thinking and practice as a writer. Barthes states that the book is not so much about his ideas as it is 'the book of my resistances to my own ideas' (RB: 119). Often this resistance involves recognizing patterns of theoretical practice in his previous works and then submitting such patterns to critical consideration. The most frequently discussed pattern is one which has been registered throughout this study so far. Barthes describes the pattern in the following way:

Everything seems to suggest that his discourse proceeds according to a two-term dialectic: popular opinion and its contrary, *Doxa* and paradox, the stereotype and the novation, fatigue and freshness, relish and disgust: *I like/ I don't like*.

(RB: 68)

The Doxa here is 'Public Opinion, the mind of the majority, petit bourgeois' (RB: 47). The whole of *Mythologies* can be said to be a critique of the *Doxa*. And yet, as Barthes notes, all his major moves as a theorist and writer seem to have come from a desire to counter the most popular and universally accepted ideas in bourgeois or what is, by the 1970s, increasingly termed mass culture. The Doxa is that which has been assimilated by majority culture and has been given the appearance of Nature. The resistance to his own ideas involves Barthes's constant attempt to stop his writing from becoming naturalized, another example of the Doxa. In the section of the text entitled 'Doxa/paradoxa' Barthes provides a condensed history of his career so far in which each approach has had ultimately to be challenged and moved beyond in order to resist the danger of naturalization. The last move he refers to concerns the rejection of the dream of a science of structuralism and its replacement by the theory of the text. However, Barthes notes that even this move courts the danger of naturalization, the danger that, left as a final position, the theory of the text will itself 'degenerate into prattle' (RB: 71).

Recognizing such a recurrent pattern in his thinking and his work necessarily provokes Barthes into a questioning of the Doxa/paradoxa opposition itself and a search for a 'third term' which would 'translate' (reposition) the opposition Doxa/paradoxa (RB: 69). What is that new translation? that 'third term'? There are many candidates in Barthes's later work for this 'third term'. In one section of *Roland Barthes* he states quite clearly that the new 'mana-word' in his work is 'the word "body"' (RB: 130). In this chapter we shall also see other important new key words entering into Barthes's theoretical vocabulary: pleasure and hedonism are noticeable examples. However, the prime candidate within *Roland Barthes* for this new 'third term' is the word *le neutre*, 'the neutral'. In a section entitled 'The Neutral', Barthes writes that the neutral is not a 'third term' which resolves the conflict between Doxa and paradoxa but 'the second term of a new paradigm, of which violence (combat, victory, theatre, arrogance) is the primary term' (RB: 132–3).

The opposition between violence and the neutral is related to Barthes's renewed analysis of the relation between language and power in the 1970s. In two essays of 1973, 'The War of Languages' and 'The Division of Languages' (RL: 106–10; 111–24), Barthes distinguishes between what he calls 'encratic' and 'acratic' language. Encratic language is the language of power and is that language which imposes itself as natural, as Doxa. Acratic language, on the other hand, involves discourses which are '*outside power*' (RL: 120). It might be difficult at first to understand how any language can be outside of power. We can best understand Barthes's point here, however, by moving to another opposition within his work.

The opposition between encratic and acratic language has relations to another important opposition between *écrivance* and *écriture*. The two terms stand for two kinds of writing, or rather, as Barthes's 1972 essay 'Outcomes of the Text' makes clear, the former should be translated in opposition to *writing*: '*écrivance* . . . is not writing [*écriture*], but its inauthentic form' (RL: 244). In *Sollers Writer*, Barthes adds that the 'only reliable way of distinguishing *l'écrivance* from *l'écriture*' is in the following way: 'When language is used to transmit ideas or information – as in l'écrivance – it can be summarized. When used for its own sake – as in l'écriture – it cannot' (SW: 84). Écriture, or writing proper, for Barthes, is language which is 'used for its own sake' and, we might add, language which considers its own condition *as language*. Écrivance, on the contrary, is language which is used as a medium to convey ideas. Écrivance, which we might gloss as *the language of the author*, is assertive, it wishes to be considered as a transparent medium for the conveyance of singular and stable meaning. In this regard, then, écrivance is the language of power; it is the language which acts on behalf of ideology: écrivance seems to correspond to encratic language, écriture to acratic language.

What do these other oppositions do to help us understand Barthes's violence/neutral opposition? Barthes refers, in *Roland Barthes*, to a common experience as a writer of looking back at the day's writing only to feel 'a kind of fear' generated by 'his sense of producing a double discourse, whose mode overreached its aim, somehow: for the aim of his discourse is not truth, and yet this discourse is assertive' (RB: 48). While intending to produce écriture or acratic writing, Barthes here finds traces of the assertive, the definitive, encratic writing (écrivance) within his day's work. He goes on:

> This kind of embarrassment started, for him, very early; he strives to master
> it – for otherwise he would have to stop writing – by reminding himself that it
> is language which is assertive, not he.
>
> (RB: 48)

Everyone surely has experienced a similar phenomenon. An example I have often noticed occurs when people ask me where I was born. The answer I give is the true one for me: *London*. Spoken as a simple, polite answer to a question, or even at times with an attempt at irony ('I live here now, although I come from London: isn't life unpredictable?'), the answer can be registered by others as the expression of a wholly unintended arrogance, sounding, in the questioner's ears, something like: 'I come from the Big Smoke!'. 'London', as a word, has an assertiveness which I am, as a speaker, often quite powerless to tame or neutralize. Language has the tendency to be assertive, violent, the apparent conveyor of truth and certainty, even when the speaker or writer intends the opposite of certainty and assertion.

The violence which Barthes pits against what he calls 'the neutral' is a violence inherent within language. Barthes's writing, when viewed in terms of his homosexuality, is a good example of what he means by neutral writing. Apart from the private journals, collected together as *Incidents*, and published seven years after his death, Barthes never writes explicitly, definitively as a gay man. Yet Barthes's homosexuality, in ways which are precisely beyond summary, hovers over and resonates through many of his major texts: *S/Z*, *Empire of Signs*, *A Lover's Discourse*, *Mythologies*, even *The Fashion System*. In a review essay on Renaud Camus's *Tricks*, Barthes, without directly involving himself as a subject, looks at homosexuality as a sociocultural phenomenon:

> Homosexuality shocks less, but continues to be interesting; it is still at that
> stage of excitation where it provokes what might be called feats of discourse.
> Speaking of homosexuality permits those who 'aren't' to show how open,
> liberal, and modern they are, and those who 'are' to bear witness, to assume
> responsibility, to militate. Everyone gets busy, in different ways, whipping
> it up.
>
> Yet, to proclaim yourself something is always to speak at the behest of a
> vengeful Other, to enter into his discourse, to argue with him, to seek from him
> a scrap of identity: 'You are . . .' 'Yes, I am . . .' Ultimately, the attribute is of no
> importance; what society will not tolerate is that I should be . . . *nothing*,

or, more precisely, that the *something* I am should be openly expressed as provisional, revocable, insignificant, inessential, in a word irrelevant. Just say 'I am,' and you will be socially saved.

(RL: 291–2)

Society, in its desire to eradicate signs of otherness or difference, wants to give a name to everything and everyone; in *Roland Barthes*, Barthes talks about this process in terms of being 'pigeonholed, assigned to an (intellectual) site, to residence in a caste' (RB: 49). Against such a process Barthes gives a description of Renaud Camus's writing which, although it does not employ the term, is clearly related to the notion of neutral writing:

Renaud Camus's *Tricks* are simple. This means that they speak homosexuality, but never speak about it: at no moment do they invoke it (that is simplicity: never to invoke, not to let Names into language – Names, the source of dispute, of arrogance, of moralizing).

(RL: 292)

Barthes seems to have grown increasingly resistant to the process whereby he was given social names, even the names of movements he had formerly promoted: structuralism, semiology, Marxism, psychoanalysis. In a 1978 essay entitled 'The Image' he speaks personally of the experience of being socially named (of being assigned an image) and compares it, rather surreally, to being fried in oil like a pomme frite. Against such a process, Barthes posits a strategy, one clearly related to his notion of neutral writing, of 'thwarting the Image', corrupting 'language, vocabularies'. 'I have gone over', Barthes declares, 'to the side of the Corrupters' (RL: 357).

We may feel that we encounter a problem in the logic of Barthes's approach here, however. There seems to be a tension in his stated position between the idea of neutral writing and the corruption of social names and images. Surely, to be a corrupter is to become involved in a process which includes a form of violence. We associate the purposeful corruption of images (the traditional term would be 'iconoclasm') with violent conduct. The resolution of this apparent tension, however, takes us to the heart of Barthes's later writing. We should remember here that violence does not refer to challenging that which is false, illusory and powerful (culture, the Doxa), but rather concerns the ideological nature of language. Ideology, by the 1970s, is for Barthes any language which depends on what he calls the 'Name' or 'Naming', a process we can translate as giving stable signifieds to signifiers. Barthes's work might be associated with Marxist and left-wing political positions. However, by the 1970s Barthes views all explicitly ideological language as partaking of the violence of the Doxa (see RB: 104). There is no sense, Barthes argues, in making distinctions between dominant ideology (from the state) and subversive ideology (resistance to the state), since all ideological language is violent and partakes of the Doxa. All ideological language is dominant (PT: 32–3). Neutral writing is not beyond conflict, in that it struggles against ideological language, the Doxa. However, Barthes increasingly stresses that such a struggle must be pitted as much against left-wing and Marxist language as it is against the language of 'dominant' culture (RB: 53).

The violence Barthes's writing is ultimately written against can perhaps best be described as language that is militant. He writes: 'Hence I suffer three arrogances: that of Science, that of the *Doxa*, that of the Militant' (RB: 47). Militantly left-wing writing, or militantly gay (nowadays the term would be 'queer') writing, is as dependent on the stereotype, the Name, the illusion of the stable and unchallengeable signified, as it is on dominant bourgeois and petit-bourgeois culture. Barthes notes that what exposes a person to scandal or notoriety in public changes, depending on whether the discourse involved is bourgeois or left-wing. Bourgeois discourse is scandalized by the exposure of 'the sexual private life', left-wing discourse is scandalized by 'traces of bourgeois ideology confessed in the subject . . . passion, friendship, tenderness, sentimentality, delight in writing' (RB: 82–3). Yet both discourses are violent, repressing certain modes of language, writing and behavior in favour of other, sanctioned and privileged modes. Bourgeois and petit-bourgeois culture share with militant left-wing and Marxist discourse a pigeonholing of the subject in forms of endoxal language: language which is frozen, imprisioning to the subject who seeks their freedom in and through textuality, écriture, a writing which is free of the stereotype.

PLEASURE/HEDONISM

Barthes's later work is fuelled by a resistance to the orthodoxies of mass culture; but, more significantly, it is written against the grain of left-

wing and Marxist orthodoxies. It presents what Barthes styles as a
'transgression of transgression'. An example of such a process, he
writes, would be allowing into one's theoretical discourse '*a touch
of sentimentality*: would that not be the *ultimate* transgression? the transgression of transgression itself. For, after all, that would be *love*:
which would return: *but in another place*' (RB: 66). In order to avoid
the Doxa of radical (left-wing) discourse, Barthes allows into his
writing themes and tones (here, love and sentimentality) which are
precisely barred by the orthodoxies of that discourse. Barthes's desire,
therefore, is to protect writing (écriture) from solidifying into Doxa,
into the Name which represses and covers over plurality and difference.
In his later work such a desire is most thoroughly associated with
taking up apparently unfashionable positions as a writer, in particular
the position of a personalized, individual, pleasure-seeking subject.
Barthes frequently associates such a (neutral) writing as one which
comes from *the body* (RB: 90). The body of the writing subject is
that, according to Barthes, which seems most scandalous to both
bourgeois and petit-bourgeois culture (with its ideas of perversity and
sexual deviance) and Marxist-inspired left-wing discourses (with their
ban on the personal, the sentimental, that which is pleasurable).
Conservative and left-wing discourses seem to conspire together to
ban the writing subject from indulging in the pleasures and perversities
of the body. To bourgeois culture such pleasures seem at best self-
indulgent and at worst sinful; to left-wing culture such pleasures
seem to involve the writer in a reactionary, bourgeois expression
of individuality, to return to a conservative belief in the subject (the
body) outside of politics. Against such orthodoxies, on the right and
the left sides of the political spectrum, Barthes defiantly takes
post-structuralist theory and directs it at his own body and his own
pleasures.

In a 1975 interview, discussing *The Pleasure of the Text*, Barthes
describes the impulse which led him to concentrate on *pleasure*:

> That word appeared in what I would call a tactical fashion. I felt that today's
> intellectual language was submitting too easily to moralizing imperatives that
> eliminated all notion of enjoyment, of bliss. In reaction, I wanted therefore to
> reintroduce this word within my personal range, to lift its censorship, to
> unblock it, to *un-repress* it.

(GV: 205)

As he states in the text itself, pleasure as a theme is meant to shock the theory of the text out of a potential solidification, to redirect that theory into areas it has previously excluded from its line of vision. Pleasure, in this sense, is seen by Barthes as a question posed to the theory of the text. He writes:

> As a trivial, unworthy name (who today would call himself a hedonist with a straight face?), it [pleasure] can embarrass the text's return to morality, to truth: to the morality of truth: it is an oblique, a drag anchor, so to speak, without which the theory of the text would revert to a centered system, a philosophy of meaning.
>
> (PT: 64–5)

In order to stop the theory of the text becoming a 'centred system' Barthes moves it, and thus himself as a writer, into the realm of hedonism.

The theory of the text articulated in *S/Z* is not repeated in *The Pleasure of the Text*; it is, rather, submitted to what we might call, following Kristeva's term, a 'transposition' (Kristeva, 1984: 59–60). The theory of the text is still recognizable in the *Pleasure of the Text*, except that it has been moved (transposed) so that we cannot simply read *S/Z* as the 'tutor text', the text that simply explains the latter text. An example comes in Barthes's famous distinction between pleasure and bliss (*plaisir* and *jouissance*). Barthes writes of two texts, the text of pleasure and the text of bliss. We cannot, however, simply translate

HEDONISM

Blackburn defines hedonism as 'the pursuit of one's pleasure as an end in itself' (Blackburn 1994: 168). Such an approach is normally viewed as unethical in that it presupposes an attention to the self at the expense of others. Many pleasures, however, can be found in socially positive activities: charitable works, friendship, even at times teaching. To capture what is normally meant by the word we would have to define hedonism as the pursuit of pleasures which are individual and either anti-social or lacking in social utility. Few philosophies have ever laid claim to hedonism as a value, therefore, and it is precisely this philosophical and ethical taboo around the concept which attracts Barthes.

such terms into the distinction between the readerly and the writerly texts presented in *S/Z*. Both pleasure and bliss have to do with writerly texts; however, it often appears that pleasure is to be found in the kind of partially reversible text exemplified by Balzac's *Sarrasine*, while bliss is reserved for modern, avant-garde texts such as those found in the work of Sollers. The reader must be careful, however, since Barthes exploits to the full the subtle shifts in his writing which make the referent of a sentence or passage at one moment kinds of texts (text of pleasure, text of bliss) and at other moments modes of reading texts (reading *as* pleasure, reading *as* bliss).

Barthes, in *The Pleasure of the Text*, finds a way of finally refusing to resolve a tension which exhibits itself throughout his work: this tension involves the apparent need to choose between classical literature and avant-garde texts. Since his text is as much about an approach to reading as about the nature of literary texts themselves, Barthes can hold in suspension his commitment to the 'freshness of language' (to the avant-garde's desire to break with literary stereotypes) at the same time as positively valuing the works of classical literature themselves. Barthes can perform such a balancing act since his new subject, pleasure, is by definition contradictory. Barthes writes at the very beginning of his text: 'who endures contradiction without shame? Now this anti-hero exists: he is the reader of the text at the moment that he takes his pleasure' (PT: 3). Pleasure, in Barthes's hedonist handling of it, resists the certainties of both the conservative and the left-wing sides of social discourse. It lies outside of intellectual theory's militant commitment to society and social reform, and yet it is also something other than conservative, academic criticism's emphasis on values such as beauty and the passive admiration of the great works of the past. Pleasure, in Barthes's account, is neutral or neuter: 'it is a drift', he writes:

> something both revolutionary and asocial, and it cannot be taken over by any collectivity, any mentality, any ideolect. Something *neuter*? It is obvious that the pleasure of the text is scandalous: not because it is immoral but because it is *atopic*.
>
> (PT: 23)

Pleasure is 'atopic' since it denies the expectations of established discourse, be they conservative or radical intellectual discourses. What is most atopic about pleasure is its anti-social, anti-collective tendency.

TOPOS

The ancient word *topos*, from which we derive the word *topic*, means 'commonplace'. A commonplace is, in classical rhetoric, both a received idea (a stereotype or cliché) but also a common place within discourse: to begin a children's story with 'Once upon a time' is to honour a well-established topos. A topos, then, is a Name in the manner in which Barthes employs that term: an established and expected element of discourse.

Barthes's reader needs to be clear on this last point, however. In distinguishing between pleasure in reading and bliss in reading Barthes sums up his contradictory position as an intellectual. Pleasure, a comfortable delight in reading, derives mainly from texts which are part of the cultural heritage: Balzac, Flaubert, Proust. Seen in this way, the pleasure afforded by such texts might seem to plug the reader into shared social values. However, bliss in reading is radically anti-social; it is a kind of experience akin to sexual climax (jouissance, Barthes's word for bliss or what at times should be translated as *ecstasy*, might be translated into modern English as 'coming'). We might associate sex with a social activity (it involves more than oneself, after all). However jouissance or coming, for Barthes, disperses or scatters the self in a moment in which, instead of finding or communicating with ourselves, we lose even ourselves:

> Text of pleasure: the text that contents, fills, grants euphoria; the text that comes from culture and does not break with it, is linked to a *comfortable* practice of reading. Text of bliss: the text that imposes a state of loss, the text that discomforts (perhaps to the point of a certain boredom), unsettles the reader's historical, cultural, psychological assumptions, the consistency of his tastes, values, memories, brings to a crisis his relation with language.
>
> (PT: 14)

The approach to the text Barthes presents in *The Pleasure of the Text* inhabits both of these apparently opposed states (the pleasure of the text, the bliss of the text) without choosing between them. The reader presented (or imagined) in Barthes's text is a self-consciously contradictory subject: 'he enjoys the consistency of his selfhood (that is, his

THE SUBJECT

Traditionally, reference to the subject involves the notion of '*the conscious or thinking subject*', the self or ego of the individual human being (Hawthorn 1992: 180–2). Philosophy since Plato has paid great attention to the subject, often positing it (like Barthes's traditional author) as the centre and origin of meaning. In structuralism, and especially post-structuralism, however, this traditional privileging of the subject comes under attack. In post-structuralist work the subject begins to be seen as something constructed either by dominant ideology or by language. Theorists following the former path are influenced by Marxist thought, in particular the work of Louis Althusser (1918–90), while those following the latter path are generally influenced by the psychoanalytical theories of Jacques Lacan (1901–81). Freud had presented a major challenge to traditional notions of the subject by developing an account of the Unconscious. In Freud, the Unconscious is at once unknown to the subject and yet is the source of that subject's actions, desires, familial and social relations. A disturbing gap or split emerges within the subject with the advent of psychoanalysis. Lacan's theories concentrate around a rereading of Freud in the light of modern linguistics and culminate in Lacan's famous assertion that the Unconscious is structured like a language. In post-structuralist theories influenced by Lacan the subject is seen as the product of language. The subject is no longer the source and origin of human action and thought, but rather a site in which language's presence is felt. This point can be reinforced by considering the nature of the grammatical Subject. In a sentence the Subject is 'a word or group of words constituting the "nominative" to a finite verb' (*OED*); the Subject governs the predicate of the sentence. In the common sentence 'I love you', the Subject is the word 'I'. Post-structuralists like Barthes are fond of asserting that there is nothing behind or beyond the subject seen in this grammatical sense. We may like to think, for example, that when we say 'I love you' we are expressing a unique and purely personal emotion (the meaning of the subject traditionally conceived). We are, however, merely repeating a necessary sentential construction: subject before predicate, predicate before object. We are also, of course, producing what is perhaps the most overused of all clichés. The subject, here, loses itself in language, is constructed by and through language. For post-structuralism all language works in this way. The source of meaning is not the human subject but language working in and through the subject.

pleasure) and seeks its loss (that is, his bliss). He is a subject split twice over, doubly perverse' (PT: 14). It is in statements such as these that Barthes begins to articulate fully what he means by hedonism. Barthes's hedonistic approach to the text is not an approach which narcissistically serves the individual subject, as left-wing intellectual theory might suppose, since it is an approach in which, at the very moment of bliss, of jouissance, the subject dissolves, is lost. As Barthes puts the issue in *Roland Barthes*: 'today the subject apprehends himself *elsewhere*, and "subjectivity" can return at another place on the spiral: deconstructed, taken apart, shifted, without anchorage: why should I not speak of "myself" since this "my" is no longer "the self"?' (RB: 168). Barthes here articulates succinctly, if densely, a major feature of post-structuralist theory: the deconstruction or dismantling of the traditional notion of the human subject.

At the end of the last chapter we saw how an avant-garde writer like Sollers plays with the pronominal subject of his sentences, shifting between first-person ('I') and third-person ('he') like the black-and-white pieces on a chessboard. The effect of such writing is to disturb the traditional notion of a singular, non-linguistic subject behind the text. Barthes uses a similar technique in *Roland Barthes*, shifting between 'I', 'he' and 'R.B.' Such pronouns are not signs of his authorial, non-linguistic presence behind the text but are, rather, what Roman Jakobson (1896–1982), a linguist and structuralist critic who was highly influential on Barthes's thinking, calls 'shifters'. The 'I' or the 'he', or indeed the proper name of the sentence, can refer to more than one referent, depending on its context. Such pronominal subjects shift their reference, creating the kind of decentred meaning, or signifiance, we saw Barthes noting in his reading of Balzac's *Sarrasine*. Barthes, in *Roland Barthes*, gives a neat, if prosaic, example of this effect when he refers to the receipt of a postcard which reads: '*Monday. Returning tomorrow. Jean-Louis*'. Barthes 'marvels at discovering in so simple an utterance the trace of those double operators, *shifters*, analyzed by Jakobson'. He goes on:

> if Jean-Louis knows perfectly well who he is and on what day he is writing, once his message is in my hands it is entirely uncertain: *which Monday? which Jean-Louis?* How would I be able to tell, since *from my point of view* I must instantly choose between more than one Jean-Louis and several Mondays? Though coded, to speak only of the most familiar of these operators, the shifter thus

appears as a complex means – furnished by language itself – of breaking
communication.

(RB: 165–6)

Bliss (jouissance), for Barthes, involves a loss of stable subjecthood
in language. It involves a moment in which the reader as subject and
the author as object dissolve into the realm of textuality: 'there is not,
behind the text', Barthes writes of this moment, 'someone active
(the writer) and out front someone passive (the reader); there is not
a subject and an object' (PT: 16). Such a moment of bliss dissolves
and disperses the reader's self into language, into textuality: it is an
'asocial' moment which does not, however, involve a 'recurrence to
the subject (subjectivity)': 'everything is lost, integrally' Barthes states
(PT: 39). The sexual, bodily metaphor of jouissance, or 'coming', is
tempered in Barthes's writing precisely towards such an experience of
loss rather than consolidation or assertion of self: 'bliss is the system
of reading, or utterance, through which the subject, instead of establishing itself, is lost, experiencing that expenditure which is, properly
speaking, bliss' (GV: 206).

The moment of bliss for the reader, it is important to note, occurs
when that reader is confronted with writing which does not reproduce
the Doxa, the stereotype. To be confronted with the Doxa, the stereotype, is to be placed in a situation in which one's subjecthood is called
into question; Barthes's comments on the discourse of homosexuality
cited earlier are a testament to this process. To be confronted with
the text of bliss is to experience, at least for Barthes, a release from the
troubling illusion of a singular subjecthood that is capable or desirous
of choice and ideological allegiance. The moment of bliss, in other
words, occurs when the subject is confronted with language that undoes
the social question of identity ('Are you? . . .'), when the subject
escapes into a language which denies the possibility of a statement of
identity ('I am . . .'). Conservative and left-wing discourses depend on
the traditional notion of the subject in order to disseminate the stereotype or Doxa. The text of bliss, however, disturbs such a process:
'What is overcome, split', by such texts, Barthes argues, 'is the *moral
unity* that society demands of every human product' (PT: 31). In many
ways, therefore, Barthes's argument in *The Pleasure of the Text* can
be related back to his first book, *Writing Degree Zero*, since the text of
bliss is, ultimately, something which presents the reader with what is

radically new (fresh, beyond cliché or repetition). The text of bliss, we might say, is a text which has not yet been acculturated and thus speaks outside of the social demand for the Name, for single identity (PT: 40–1). One of the major differences between Barthes's account of the 'new' here and in *Writing Degree Zero*, however, is the recognition that every text of bliss is so only in the present moment in which it is read. Taking up the emphasis placed on the reader's production of the text in works such as *S/Z*, Barthes here stresses that the text of bliss (and thus the experience of bliss in relation to a text) is unrepeatable, can only occur in a present time outside of history or any systematic language. Barthes's view of the avant-garde is clear: 'the avant-garde is that restive language which is going to be recuperated' (PT: 54). But what is also clear in such a theory is how far Barthes himself has moved from any attempt to produce a general, methodological, communicable model of reading. Barthes's bodily, pleasure-filled, occasionally orgasmic account of reading in *The Pleasure of the Text* is as far away as one can imagine from the structuralist ideal of a science of literature, or indeed from any theoretical position one might call general. Barthes's work of the 1970s, with its emphasis on a mode of writing which attempts to avoid the violence of the Doxa and the Name, challenges our very sense of what 'theoretical' writing is, since it begins to occupy a place in which distinctions between kinds of writing (fictional and non-fictional, novelistic and critical) break down.

A NOVELISTIC TEXT?

In a 1978 essay on Proust, Barthes wonders whether he will eventually leave theory behind in favour of the writing of a novel (RL: 289) and there has been a good deal of speculation about how far Barthes's plans (or at least desire) to write his 'utopian novel' had developed by the time of his death. What can be known for sure, however, is that Barthes in the latter part of his life began to distinguish clearly between the traditional novel genre and a form of writing he called the 'novelistic'. In a 1973 interview, playing on the meaning of the word *essay* in terms of *a test* or *an experiment*, Barthes states that: 'my writings are already full of the novelistic' (GV: 176). Barthes rather famously asserts, at the beginning of his *Roland Barthes*, that: 'It must all be considered as if spoken by a character in a novel' (RB: 1). In a 1975 interview he describes *Roland Barthes* in the following way:

It's a novel, but not a biography. The detour is not the same. It's intellectually novelistic – novelistic for two reasons. First of all, many of the fragments concern the novelistic surface of life, and in addition, what is presented or staged in these fragments is an image-repertoire; i.e., the very discourse of the novel. . . . The book's discourse is novelistic rather than intellectual . . .

(GV: 223)

If there can be degrees of such a concept, then Barthes's *Fragments d'un discours amoureux* (1977), translated in English as *A Lover's Discourse: Fragments*, is the most novelistic of all his works. The clue to that text's novelistic quality as writing comes in Barthes's use in the quotation above of the term *image-repertoire*.

Barthes's *Lover's Discourse* is structured around eighty figures arranged in alphabetical order. These figures arise in the mind of the amorous subject like 'the printout of a code'; they are the intertextual elements of the lover's discourse. Barthes writes that 'the amorous subject draws on the reservoir (the thesaurus?) of figures, depending on the needs, the injunctions, or the pleasures of his image-repertoire' (LD: 6).

The fundamental irony of the amorous subject is already contained in these observations. Love, that supposedly most personal of emotions, is experienced by the subject in terms of the emergence of scraps of code deriving from something as general and impersonal as a thesaurus, a dictionary even. The reason the subject does not immediately recognize this irony, that his or her apparently personal responses are part of a general lexicon of figures, involves the psychoanalytical background of the idea of the 'image-repertoire'.

THE IMAGE-REPERTOIRE

The image-repertoire is Barthes's version of Lacan's term *l'imaginaire*, the Imaginary, a concept related to Lacan's most famous revision of Freud, 'the mirror stage'.

In episode after unconnected episode or, to use Barthes's term, incident after unconnected incident, Barthes presents the image-repertoire or Imaginary of the amorous subject. The lover's discourse, which is always directed at the 'you', the beloved object, is a text, a weave of intertextual traces from literature, psychology, philosophy, religion, music and personal experience. Yet we might ask the question, if this discourse is part of the Imaginary, a fiction which Barthes at one point

THE IMAGINARY AND THE MIRROR STAGE

In Lacan's essay, known in its abbreviated form as 'The Mirror Stage' (Lacan 1989: 1–7), the human child begins without a sense of self or even of the differences between its own body and the other bodies around it. The child's body at this stage, as Elizabeth Grosz puts it, is 'an uncoordinated, discrete assemblage of parts exhibiting no regulated organization or internal cohesion' (Grosz: 44). 'The mirror stage' is Lacan's term for the manner in which the child comes to assemble a sense of unity of self. This sense of a unified self or ego comes from others, either the reflected image of the self in the mirror or the body of the mother. The crucial point is that the unified ego or self is predicated on an image (something other, outside of, the still dependent and uncoordinated body of the child). As Lacan states: 'the important point is that this form situates the agency of the ego, before its social determination, in a fictional direction, which will always remain irreducible for the individual alone ...' (Lacan 1989: 2). The mirror stage, therefore, begins that process in which we imagine (on the basis of an internalized image) that we are unified in our bodies and unified as subjects in time. The Imaginary, therefore, involves the fiction we have of ourselves as a unified subject, the greatest part of the fiction resting in the fact that we construct this idea of a unified self from images outside of ourselves, from Otherness. There is a great loss or gap in the Imaginary, therefore: our image of ourselves seems to be fictional and to be based on loss or a gap in our selves. Society, of course, radically intensifies this gap in our adult lives by offering us a host of images upon which to constitute our fictions of self. It would be possible, on this basis, to analyse the Imaginary of the housewife, the businessman, the professor, the movie star, the politician, the social rebel and, as Barthes does, the lover.

compares to madness (LD: 121), why does Barthes write a text which is apparently motivated by a desire to defend it? Barthes begins his text by noting that the lover's discourse 'is spoken, perhaps, by thousands of subjects . . . but warranted by no one: it is completely forsaken by the surrounding languages: ignored, disparaged, or derided by them'. He goes on to argue that it is precisely because of this social exile that the lover's discourse becomes a possible site for 'affirmation': 'That affirmation is', he adds, 'the subject of the book which begins here' (LD: 1).

We have spent some time in this chapter remarking on the manner in which Barthes, in his later work, purposefully takes up positions and themes which are sidelined by radical intellectual theory. Even with such knowledge, however, the logic of this opening passage might strike us as less than evident. Is it really the case that a discourse which has been forsaken needs to be affirmed? Could it not be the case that the lover's discourse has been forsaken purely and simply because it *is* 'unreal'? It could certainly be argued that it is by encouraging us to fall in love (to fall into the Imaginary of the loving subject) that society is able to divert our energies, energies which could otherwise be employed in more rebellious actions. It is almost indisputable that the discourse of love allows modern capitalism to turn us into compliant consumers.

Why does Barthes write a text which seeks to affirm the lover's discourse? The first point that needs to be made with regard to such a question is that Barthes's lover, the figure who says 'I' in his text, does not experience love as an affirmation but as a loss, a series of frustrations, anxieties, suspensions, anticipations and neurotic quests after an always elusive positive meaning to trivial signs. Barthes's lover is a reader of signs, a semiotician in love (as many, if not all, lovers are), who constantly searches for signs that the other (the beloved) participates in the Imaginary, the fiction of the lover's self. However, since the loved one is Other to the lover's Imaginary, such a quest for positive signs can only lead to inevitable disappointment, frustration and loss.

The incessant search for signs of requited love (one might say signs of a shared image-repertoire) is matched by the lover's need to present signs of his love, to convince the loved one, or the image of the loved one, that the lover's Imaginary is real or, rather, connected to the 'Real':

> I make myself cry, in order to prove to myself that my grief is not an illusion: tears are signs, not expressions. By my tears, I tell a story, I produce a myth of grief, and henceforth I adjust myself to it: I can live with it, because, by weeping, I give myself an emphatic interlocutor who receives the 'truest' of messages, that of my body, not of my speech.

> (LD: 182)

The amorous subject, the 'I' of Barthes's text, is a character in his own novel; or rather, the 'I' of *A Lover's Discourse* is a character in a novel (of unrequited love, of the frustration of the Imaginary coming up against the Real) who wishes to be a character in another novel (in which the Imaginary becomes the Real). Barthes, in an interview, talks about his decision not to write 'a treatise on amorous discourse'; this, he says, 'would have been a kind of lie (I no longer aspired to any claims of scientific generality for my work)'. In the place of such a treatise, Barthes chose to write a 'feigned', 'fabricated' 'discourse of *a* lover. Who is not necessarily myself'. 'The result', Barthes goes on to say, is: 'a composed, feigned, or, if you prefer, a "pieced-together" discourse (the result of montage)' (GV: 284–5).

A Lover's Discourse is a novelistic text. It is a text which presents a fictional character (intertexually compiled out of pieces of literary, philosophical, experiential and other kinds of discourse) whose condition it is to live in a novelistic fiction wishing that they lived in another kind of fiction. The results of such a text are complex. On one level, Barthes's writing of the lover's discourse fully exposes the illusory, mythological nature of the discourse of love. At the same moment, however, Barthes's text treats its character (the discourse of love, the 'I' that says 'I love you') with love, affirms it, retrieves it from its intellectual rejection. The result is to present a text which demonstrates the fictional, deluded nature of amorous discourse while avoiding the violence of an explicit demythologizing critique. *A Lover's Discourse* is an embodiment of Barthes's neutral writing and the contradictions such a writing embraces: suspended between a militant language which would debunk the lover's discourse and a conservative language which would sentimentalize and naturalize it, the text presents its reader with a disturbing yet pleasurable mirror. The reader of *A Lover's Discourse* identifies with the implicit critique of a major cultural myth at the same time that they identify with the 'I' (the character) who speaks the discourse of that myth. The result is that we are challenged in our own relation to the discourse of love without being offered the consolation of a definitive, objective theory of that discourse.

SUMMARY

Barthes's work of this period shows him moving to a form of writing which, while still informed by radical theoretical ideas and positions, resists method and begins to disturb the boundary between fictional and non-fictional writing. Increasingly conscious of the stereotypical and thus repetitive nature of radical political and intellectual discourse, Barthes explores modes of writing which refuse to counter the Doxa (naturalized language) with a paradoxical demystification. Incorporating unfashionable subjects like love, sentiment and pleasure into his writing, Barthes pushes the theory of the text into a more bodily realm, a hedonistic pleasure of the text. Such developments lead to modes of writing that are better described as novelistic than theoretical.

8

MUSIC AND
PHOTOGRAPHY

Many readers whose first priority is the visual rather than the literary arts come to Barthes through his work on photography and cinema. Barthes's work on music is highly significant to those working within that field. This chapter looks at Barthes's contribution to these areas and in so doing prepares the ground for the next chapter's examination of Barthes's last book, *Camera Lucida*.

THE GRAIN OF THE VOICE: BARTHES ON MUSIC

In the 1970s Barthes wrote a number of essays on music which incorporate the key concepts of his work of this period and in so doing offer an illuminating and fresh perspective on those concepts. 'Musica Practica', published in 1970, is a good example. In this essay Barthes promotes a view of music as performance which can be clearly related to the major arguments of *S/Z*. Depreciating the increasing cultural tendency to consume professional music in a recorded form, Barthes promotes an active engagement with music which clearly relates to his theories of the writerly text. Barthes asks: 'What is the use of composing if it merely confines the product in the enclosure of the concert or the solitude of radio reception? To compose is, at least by tendency, to offer for *doing*, not to offer for hearing but for writing' (RF: 265).

Such a distinction, between active performance of a musical score and passive consumption of a musical performance, leads in later essays of the decade into a privileging of the amateur as opposed to the professional. Barthes was, from his early childhood, a dedicated amateur musician. Various essays of the latter part of the decade, many of them oriented towards a positive assessment of the music of Robert Alexander Schumann (1810–56), promote an amateur performance of music which has clear relations to Barthes's theories of the productive, reversible reading of texts. Barthes writes in his 1979 essay 'Loving Schumann': 'nowadays listening to music is dissociated from its practice: many virtuosos, listeners, *en masse*: but as for practictioners, amateurs – very few' (RF: 294).

In *The Pleasure of the Text* Barthes had commented on the sad fact that, according to official statistics, only half of the French nation nowadays read books. This fact is a regrettable one for Barthes, but not because of the usual bourgeois moralistic notions of the edifying nature of reading. It is not to be regretted that people are less and less exposed to literature's apparent moral lessons, but rather that more and more people are alienated from the bodily, potentially ecstatic pleasures of the text. Barthes's promotion of active reading mirrors his remarks on the performance of music. His celebration of an amateur production of music is, similarly, concerned with a bodily, engaged, active relation to music which is pitted against the increasing commodification of art in a mass culture. The mass culture of recorded music and professional performances aired through national, and now global, media (such as radio and television) threatens to produce a purely passive reception of music. It also threatens to eradicate music's equivalent to what Barthes calls signifiance. Signifiance provides the reader or musical performer/listener with a signifier, rather than a clear signified; it demands a bodily, active response rather than a passive reception of an already stable and, if we can use this term, 'packaged' meaning.

Barthes explains on a number of occasions what he means by signifiance in music by comparing two singers. Charles Panzera, a 'singer of French art songs' popular between the two world wars, had given Barthes singing lessons in the late 1930s. Panzera, unfortunately, 'stopped singing at the very advent of the long-playing record' (RF: 280). In contrast, the professional singer Dietrich Fischer-Dieskau was a dominant force in the post-war era of recorded classical music.

Fischer-Dieskau's singing voice, Barthes argues, is professionalized, 'expressive, dramatic, *emotionally clear*' and thus is perfectly suited to a culture which wants its music as a product. Barthes writes:

> this culture, defined by the extension of listening and the disappearance of practice (no more amateur performers), is eager for art, for music, provided that such art and such music be clear, that they 'translate' an emotion and represent a signified (the poem's 'meaning'): an art which vaccinates enjoyment (by reducing it to a known, coded emotion) and reconciles the subject with what, in music, *can be said*: with what is said of it, predicatively, by the Academy, by Criticism, by Opinion.
>
> (RF: 273)

Fischer-Dieskau provides a signified, a musical performance which conveys the professional and cultural idea of music perfectly. In this sense his singing communicates the Doxa, the general opinion of what music is and should be. There is no room in such a form of music for the signifier, for signifiance viewed as a pleasurable, at times blissful production of music in the listener. Panzera's art of singing, on the contrary, does provide signifiance, a quality that in music Barthes terms 'the grain of the voice'.

For Barthes the grain of the voice comes from the singer's or musician's body. It is a concept which emerges from the general valorization of the bodily text which we noted in the last chapter. Barthes defines the concept through a distinction between the pheno-text and the geno-text taken from the work of Julia Kristeva. The grain of the voice, for Barthes, is precisely this language of the body (geno-text) which modern, professionalized music seeks to eradicate from its performance. Barthes's focus on this concept in music, while important in itself, also helps us to recognize the connections between his writing on literature and his work on photography. The connection involves a developing concern with elements of the text which emerge from and affect the body. Such elements cannot be contained within or captured by textual structures or within critical methodologies. They constitute a surplus or supplement which lie precisely outside of all available structures.

PHENO-TEXT AND GENO-TEXT

Kristeva's distinction between pheno-text and geno-text goes some way to explain what Barthes means by the bodily text. In Kristeva's work of the late 1960s and early 1970s she distinguishes between the Symbolic and the Semiotic. The Symbolic, a concept taken from Lacan, is discourse which is logical, involved in clear communication, and which, therefore, is the language of dominant society. The psychological subject for Kristeva, however, is split between this language and a bodily relation to language which stems from the early phases of childhood, before the subject has learnt the official languages of society. Before entering into the Symbolic Order, the child-subject is a site of drives, impulses and bodily rhythms. This is the Semiotic (le sémiotique) and, for Kristeva, it remains the great resource for what she calls the poetic. Radical literature and art (Kristeva's poetic language) attempts to tap into the Semiotic and thus puncture the transparent, naturalized and repressive language of the Symbolic. The conflict between the Symbolic and the Semiotic is registered in terms of an attack on logic, the rupture of official genres and discourses through rhythmic and other pre-logical modes of expression (see Kristeva 1984). In Kristeva's opposition, the pheno-text is that part of a text which communicates through and abides by the languages of the Symbolic Order. The geno-text is that part of some texts which can be felt through the pheno-text, puncturing, rupturing and disturbing the clear passage of communication. No text can directly present the geno-text or the force of the Semiotic, since this is a force which is prior to language itself. The geno-text can, however, be felt in certain texts which resist the dominance of the Symbolic Order.

PHOTOGRAPHY AND THE THIRD MEANING

Barthes's early work on photography can be read in relation to the critique of naturalized codes in his *Mythologies*. Essays such as 'The Photographic Message' (1961) and 'Rhetoric of the Image' (1964) attempt to apply to photographic images Barthes's semiological approach to cultural myths. The key problem for Barthes in such an application is that the photograph does not appear to produce its messages in the same manner as other, text-dependent cultural messages. There is, as Barthes notes, something revolutionary about

THE REFERENT

The referent is a problematic and much discussed concept in modern linguistics. It concerns what a sign or group of signs refer to: the referent of the word 'tree', for example, would be the actual tree or trees to which the sign 'tree' referred. We have already seen, however, that after Saussure the referential idea of language, the idea that language does actually, directly and naturally refer to things in the world, is viewed as mistaken. The sign, as we saw in Chapter 3, is arbitrary. There is no actual (necessary, natural) referential relation between the sign 'tree' and actual things in the world we call trees. It should be noted, however, that rejecting the idea of a direct (natural, necessary) referentiality in words does not mean that language cannot (conventionally, even systematically) refer to things in the world. The words in this book, for example, refer to a number of things in the world. The point is that the referentiality we are talking about here is conventional rather than natural, arbitrary rather than necessary, mediated rather than literal. Barthes's lifelong critique of analogy stems from this recognition of the arbitrary nature of language. Barthes's semiological procedure in works such as *Mythologies* and *The Fashion System* could be described in the following way: a critique of presumed analogies; a demonstration that the apparent referent of signs and sign-systems is always cultural rather than natural; a demonstration that the referent is always somewhere else than it is believed to be; and, finally, a demonstration that the referent is constructed and ideological rather than natural.

the photograph in the history of human signs. This revolutionary element concerns the photograph's apparent production of a '*message without a code*' (RF: 5). Text-based messages, Barthes argues, depend upon analogy, an apparent correspondence or comformity between signs and their referent.

Photography presents a potential problem for Barthes in his semiological phase, however, in that photographs do seem, unlike other signs, to have an actual referent. Other signs depend on a code, a movement between denotative and connotative meaning. In such signs what is presented as the referent is actually the denotative message which allows for the often implicit communication of a connotative message. Such signs are coded because they have at least two levels of meaning or signification. Photographs, on the other hand, seem to present us with a referent which is not coded. How can we argue that what is presented in a photograph is merely a denotative message which conceals a connotative message? Surely, what is presented in a photograph exists or existed in precisely the manner in which it is captured by the camera? Surely, therefore, what a photograph presents is a referent in the strictest sense of the term? All other arts, it would seem, generate or create their referent. Even apparently 'realist' forms of art, as we have seen, rely on the available codes and conventions to produce the illusion of a literal referent. Photography, however, seems merely to capture, without creating it in a new form, the literal referent it then represents as a photographic image. The photographic image (referent) seems uncoded in that it has not been created (in and through the codes of an artificial form) but merely captured. It is an image, apparently, without a code.

We have, in fact, already seen Barthes finding coded messages (connotative meanings) within photographs. In *Mythologies* Barthes's discussion of the photograph of the young French soldier does more than simply demonstrate the codedness of such an image, it also demonstrates that it is precisely in the strength of such an image's denotative power that ideology does its naturalizing work. In 'Rhetoric of the Image' Barthes presents another telling demythologizing reading of the use of a photographic image in an analysis of an advertisement for the Panzani food company. Such an advertisement deploys the referent, the pure denotative message of the image, to naturalize its cultural and ideological meanings:

> the denoted image naturalizes the symbolic message, it makes 'innocent' the very dense (especially in advertising) semantic artifice of connotation; although the Panzani poster is full of 'symbols,' there nonetheless remains in the photograph a kind of natural *being-there* of the objects, insofar as the literal message is sufficient: nature seems to produce the represented scene quite spontaneously ... the absence of a code de-intellectualizes the message because it seems to institute in nature the signs of culture.
>
> (RF: 34)

The Panzani advertisement is extremely coded: it assembles together packets of pasta and rice, tins of sauce, and natural products such as vegetables, and places them in an open string-bag out of which these products (cultural and natural) seem to be pouring (for the image itself, see IMT: image XVII). It is not difficult to register the connotations of Naturalness, Health, Italianicity (as Barthes calls it) in such an image. However, it is also true that these objects existed in this formation as they were being photographed. Like the image of the young French soldier, the connotations of the image can also be naturalized by reference to their literal, referential existence.

Barthes's response to the apparent uncoded nature of the photographic image (its pure denotation) is complex and has at least two discernible aspects. The first aspect can be said to involve the extreme care with which Barthes treats the question of the photographic referent: in short, he takes care to treat the question as a question. He repeatedly refers to the idea of the literal (uncoded) photographic referent as a myth, something commonly assumed rather than a fact about photography (RF: 7, 21). Barthes, in 'Rhetoric of the Image', takes great pains to explain that even if we could establish a literal level of the photographic image, this would not concern what people commonly mean by the literal referent. The common or 'mythical' assumption is that photographs present us with the literal object itself, what Barthes calls the *'being-there'* of the object. However, as Barthes makes clear, all images, however coded, can be said to testify to the *being-there* of the object they represent. We presume the *being-there* of the object of a drawing from life, no matter how stylized that drawing may be. It is not that the photographic image is a better or purer mode of representation than, say, drawing, painting or cinema; rather, the photographic image has its uniqueness in the fact that it presents an image that once existed as it is represented. The photographic image, in this sense, presents us with what Barthes calls the *'having-been-there'* of the object. The photographic image, that is to say, seems to have a denotative or literal *thereness*, but it is always in the past, before the time of its viewing. Barthes writes:

it is on the level of this denoted message or message without a code that we can fully understand the photograph's *real unreality*; its unreality is that of the *here*, for the photograph is never experienced as an illusion, it is in no way a *presence*, and we must deflate the magical character of the photographic image; and its reality is that of *having-been-there*, for in every photograph there is the always stupefying evidence of: *this is how it was*: we then possess, by some precious miracle, a reality from which we are sheltered.

(RF: 33)

Barthes's comments here suggest a problem far more complex than the question of whether photographs are literal in their mode of representation, and they open up questions of the temporality (relation to time) of photography which will play a major part in *Camera Lucida*.

The second aspect of Barthes's approach to the question of photography and the referent concerns the manner in which semiology allows him to avoid a hasty or simplistic resolution of the question. Since the focus of semiology is on the manner in which culture employs images and texts to convey ideological (second-order) meanings, Barthes can direct most of his efforts into analyzing how the apparent literal level of photographic images are utilized for the purpose of generating second-order meanings, or connotations. Thus, the need to resolve the question is lessened for Barthes, since his focus is directed primarily at the manner in which photographs are used rather than what they are in essence. Barthes's emphasis in this period of his work, in other words, is on the myth surrounding the idea of analogy and reference, rather than on whether purely analogical messages actually exist.

The question of the referent in photography comes back in a different form when we move on to Barthes's later work. In his essay 'The Third Meaning: Research Notes on Several Eisenstein Stills' (1970) Barthes's concern has shifted from a strictly semiological focus to one which bears the hallmarks of his celebration of the reversible text in *S/Z*. Barthes here looks at stills from films such as *Battleship Potemkin* and *Ivan the Terrible* by the Russian film-maker Sergei Eisenstein (1898–1948). The theory of the text elaborated in *S/Z* and developed in *The Pleasure of the Text* provides an illuminating framework for reading this essay. Barthes signaled on a number of occasions his preference for photography over cinema (see, for example, RL: 345–9). Cinema for Barthes seems to equate to the readerly, irreversible text. Its dependence on the narrative codes and the manner in which it generates a passive identification in its viewers make cinema a medium which, for Barthes, has little relation to the radically plural text, to signifiance and thus to a productive, potentially blissful (re)writing on the part of the audience (for a good discussion of Barthes on cinema, see Burgin 1996: 161–76, reprinted in Rabaté 1997: 19–31). Isolating stills (individual frames) from Eisenstein's films, however, allows Barthes, paradoxically, to locate what he calls the 'filmic' within Eisenstein's work. It seems that for Barthes the 'filmic' must resist chronology, narrative and the development of character and plot which most commentators would describe as the essence of filmic or cinematic art. What Barthes means by the 'filmic', however, is something which functions like the radical textuality of avant-garde literature, resisting narrative and chronology and involving the reader in a pleasurable, open, unending engagement with the signifier and thus signifiance.

Barthes's way of describing the 'filmic' element of Eisenstein's stills is to distinguish three levels of meaning within them. The informational level of the still involves what it directly communicates. The symbolic level of meaning involves the reader or viewer in the more complicated social symbolisms involved in a still. In the still from *Ivan the Terrible* with which Barthes begins his analysis, for example, the young tsar's head is showered with gold by two courtiers. The symbolic level of such a still involves a complex array of symbolic codes operating within society: gold as a sign of wealth, of initiation, of social exchange. These symbolic levels of meaning are obviously the connotative meanings of the still in question and they can all be named and discussed through the semiological method of reading developed by Barthes in the 1960s.

Barthes does not finish his reading of such images at this level of symbolic meaning, however. He calls the symbolic meaning we have just referred to the 'obvious meaning' and contrasts it to what he calls the 'obtuse meaning'. In the still in question Barthes notes that there are certain features which strike the viewer without apparently amounting to a nameable symbol or second-order connotation: one of the courtiers has thick and the other smooth and pale make-up, one has a 'stupid' nose while the other has delicate eyelids, one has hair which looks like a wig. These signs, which the viewer does not know how to read, form the 'obtuse' or 'third meaning'. Barthes notes that the word 'obtuse' 'means *blunted*, *rounded*', and goes on to suggest that such features cause his reading of the *obvious* meaning to '*skid*' (RF: 44).

The recognition of this third or obtuse meaning turns these stills from Eisenstein into a text of pleasure and even of bliss. They allow for a reading which escapes narrative and chronology and, more importantly, escapes any structure which a strictly semiological reading would find within the image. Such an unstructurable, unassimilable meaning exists only on the level of the signifier (there is no signified to finish and complete this meaning); this is a meaning, therefore, which opens up the radical play of signifiance. As Barthes writes: 'the third meaning, which we can locate theoretically but not describe, then appears as the transition from language to signifying [signifiance] and as the founding act of the filmic itself' (RF: 59).

Barthes's most sustained analysis of the third or obtuse meaning within photographic images comes in *Camera Lucida* (1980). However, the problem of the photographic referent, which we argued was deferred in Barthes's earlier essays on photography, also makes a return in this analysis.

SUMMARY

In his various essays on music Barthes elaborates upon themes already established in works such as *The Pleasure of the Text*. In particular, musical performance allows Barthes to develop his account of textual signifiance which, in this context, he refers to in terms of 'the grain of the voice'. Barthes's early work on photography and the use of the photographic image in advertising forms part of his general semiological analysis of cultural signs and myths. The problematic issue of the apparently natural or literal referent in the photographic image is rigorously examined in his semiological work, but is also maintained as a question for further examination.

9

CAMERA LUCIDA

The impossible text

Barthes's mother, Henriette Barthes, died on 25 October 1977. The impact of the loss of his mother, with whom he had lived for most of his life, can be registered in almost everything Barthes wrote between the day of her death and his own untimely death less than three years later. *Camera Lucida*, however, is a book directly about his mother and the impact upon him of her death. In offering what appears to be a theory of the essence of the photographic image, Barthes builds a loving, devastated tribute to the person who was without doubt the greatest object and source of love throughout his life.

STUDIUM AND PUNCTUM

Barthes's book is divided into two parts. The first part is involved with a theory of photography; the second part applies that theory to photographs of his family, and his mother in particular. The result of these conflicting objectives – a theory of photography, the work of mourning for the mother – produces a text which can confuse readers and which can only be understood if we return to the themes of the Chapter 7. *Camera Lucida*, while different in many ways to *Roland Barthes* and *A Lover's Discourse*, has something of the novelistic about it. It is certainly a text which blends the discourse or language of method (theory) with a wholly personal discourse (of mourning) and thus unsettles and disturbs the very results it seems to present. As Nancy Shawcross puts it: Barthes's writing in *Camera Lucida* 'simultaneously confirms and confutes one's sense that the essay is universal but also singular, that is, a discourse on photography in general and a eulogy of sorts for his mother' (Shawcross 1997: 80). The text extends Barthes's 'neutral' approach in his later writing by directly incorporating (and perhaps contaminating) theory with mourning, a general methodological account of photography with an emotional, subjective 'reflection' (in the French Barthes uses the word 'note') on a few family, and some public, photographs. How are we supposed to respond to the theory of the photographic image presented in this text once we have recognized the deeply personal event (the death of the mother) upon which it is based?

The play between general, theoretical discourse and personal emotion or bodily response is encapsulated within the very theory which Barthes presents in his book. Translating the terms of his essay 'The Third Meaning' into a new vocabulary, Barthes distinguishes between what he calls the 'studium' and the 'punctum' of a photograph. The studium of a photograph corresponds to the obvious symbolic meaning; it is something that all viewers of the image can agree upon since it presents meanings which are culturally coded. In Koen Wessing's photograph of a war-torn Nicaraguan street in 1979, the studium concerns the connotations which are established by the juxtaposition of armed soldiers, a street largely reduced to rubble, and two nuns who just happen to be passing the piece of street which Wessing is photographing. The implications of ordinary life in the midst of war, of the possible relation between war and official religion, or the juxtaposition of general cultural signs of violence and of peace, are not difficult for the reader of the image to discern, since they are part of a collective social symbolism. This photograph is, as Barthes suggests, purely concerned with the studium. The punctum, on the other hand, disturbs this obvious meaning in photographs and clearly corresponds to the third or obtuse meaning which Barthes had discussed in his earlier essay on Eisenstein. The punctum, Barthes argues, concerns an element, or number of elements, which pierce the viewer, shooting out of the image 'like an arrow'. The punctum *punctuates* the meaning of the photograph (the studium) and, as a result, punctures or pierces its viewer: 'A photograph's *punctum* is that accident which pricks me (but also bruises me, is poignant to me)' (CL: 27). It is not difficult to relate these terms to the theory of the text. The studium is read in ways which relate it to the readerly text; it concerns the clear communication of cultural codes which lead, ultimately, to a signified or set of signifieds (a stable meaning) for the image. The punctum, on the other hand, remains on the level of the signifier, lying precisely outside of shareable codes and thus a general description. The punctum is that in the picture which disturbs the image's signification and produces, for the individual reader of the image, the bliss of a reversible signifiance beyond scientific or general theoretical communication. As Barthes puts it: 'The *studium* is ultimately always coded, the *punctum* is not. . . . What I can name cannot really prick me. The incapacity to name is a good symptom of disturbance' (CL: 51).

There is a problem with the distinction between studium and punctum, however, as many commentators have noted. Barthes includes a number of photographs in *Camera Lucida*, commenting each time on where he finds the punctum. In William Klein's picture of street children in New York, it is one of the boy's bad teeth; in James Van Der Zee's 'Family Portrait', it is the strapped pumps of the 'solacing Mammy' figure; in Lewis H. Hines's photograph of two children in a New Jersey institution, it is the boy's Danton collar and the bandaged finger of the girl. The problem with all these examples is that, as Derek Attridge has noted, if Barthes is successful in convincing his readers of the presence of the punctum in these apparently insignificant details, then the details cease to be of the order of the punctum and become signs which are socially communicable: the studium (Attridge 1997: 81–3). The punctum must be that which is precisely incommunicable since once something is capable of being communicated it must be subsumed under the heading of the studium.

Barthes himself is aware of this problem, as we have already noted, by citing the passage from the conclusion of Part One of the study: 'What I can name cannot really prick me' (CL: 51). Although the two terms have been hotly contested by critics and commentators, Barthes gives them up at the beginning of the second part of his study. This part of the study moves towards a new definition of the punctum based on the discovery of a photograph of his mother at the age of five. In this one photograph, after having looked through a host of more recent photographs, Barthes finally discovers an image of his mother which, he states, conveys her 'essence'. Barthes's account of finding the Winter Garden Photograph, as he calls it, is the emotional, and perhaps also the theoretical, centre of the whole text. In extremely personal and painfully honest language, Barthes recounts first finding the photograph and then explains the essence that it captures for him.

The discovery of the Winter Garden Photograph prompts Barthes to reformulate his notion of the punctum; he decides, in fact, as he puts it: 'to 'derive' all Photography (its 'nature') from the only photograph which assuredly existed for me, and to take it somehow as a guide for my last investigation' (CL: 73). This decision leads to a very definite result, a new definition of the photographic punctum, but it is also a peculiarly defiant and illogical act. We need to be clear on the peculiarity of Barthes's decision if we are to avoid some of the more literalistic and mistaken responses the text has generated since its publication.

UNREPEATABLE THEORY

Barthes's argument, as we have seen, comes to an impasse at the end of the first part of the book: this impasse is created by the fact that a theory of the punctum within a photographic image cannot be the subject of a general theory without the loss of its uniqueness as a punctum. With this impasse in mind Barthes begins his second section, in which he moves to the personal realm, in search of a definitive image of his mother. Believing that he has discovered this definitive image, Barthes decides to base a theory of all photography upon it. The result, often missed by the book's commentators, is that Barthes's new theory of photography is self-consciously based upon the very impasse that disallowed the theory established in Part One. Barthes defiantly presents a new theory on a basis which he has already shown is unable to support a general theory of photography. The theory presented in Part Two of *Camera Lucida* is, then, precisely impossible; but, more importantly, it is self-consciously presented as impossible. As Jacques Derrida notes in his 'The Deaths of Roland Barthes', the impossibility we are speaking of here is not simply the communication of a uniquely personal (bodily) experience in general terms: more crucially, for Barthes, it involves speaking of his mother without his descriptions of her turning into a general symbolism of *the* Mother figure. How can Barthes, that is to say, write about his mother without his readers generalizing his comments; without his readers placing Barthes and his mother into general social categories? (Derrida 2001: 45–6). How can

Barthes write about his own mother without the referent of his writing turning, for his readers, into an archetype of every mother (*the* Mother)?

Many elements of Barthes's text alert us to the impossibility of the theory he is presenting. Barthes describes the Winter Garden Photograph in the following way: 'it achieved for me, utopically, *the impossible science of the unique being*' (CL: 71). He talks of his mother's last days and how, nursing her in her sickbed, she had become, figuratively, his child:

> Ultimately I experienced her, strong as she had been, my inner law, as my feminine child . . . . I who had not procreated, I had, in her very illness, engendered my mother.
>
> (CL: 72)

We remember here that the Winter Garden Photograph is of the mother as a five-year-old child. The photograph is not, in fact, included within the text, a fact which has led Diana Knight, in a compelling and highly persuasive argument, to suggest that it does not, in fact, exist and that Barthes's descriptions of it are actually of a private photograph which Barthes entitles 'The Stock' and does include in the text (see Diana Knight, 1997a: 244–69 and 1997b: 132–43). Certainly, Barthes's explanation for the omission of the Winter Garden Photograph is revealing:

> I cannot reproduce the Winter Garden Photograph. It exists only for me. For you, it would be nothing but an indifferent picture, one of the thousand manifestations of the 'ordinary'; it cannot in any way constitute the visible object of a science; it cannot establish an objectivity, in the positive sense of the term; at most it would interest your *studium*: period, clothes, photogeny; but in it, for you, no wound.
>
> (CL: 73)

The theory Barthes elaborates upon the personal, incommunicable basis of the Winter Garden Photograph returns us to the issue of the photographic referent. Unlike the image in written texts or even in painting, Barthes argues, 'in Photography I can never deny that *the thing has been there*' (CL: 76). The photograph is 'co-natural with its referent', which is to say that it has not been created by the medium which represents it. There are, of course, great problems with such an argument. Comparing Barthes's essay with the art photography of Christian Boltanski (1944–), Marjorie Perloff demonstrates how in Boltanski's photography, what appears to be the literal referent is quite frequently not what it seems. Boltanski's *10 portraits photographiques de Christian Boltanski, 1946–1964* (1972) appears to be a series of photographs depicting the photographer in different stages of boyhood. The whole set of photographs in this series, however, were shot on a single day. Indeed, Boltanski's whole procedure as a photographer is aimed at demonstrating the fact that '*photography lies . . . . it doesn't speak the truth but rather the cultural code*' (Perloff 1997: 42).

Barthes's argument is, however, somewhat more complicated than simply asserting the literal referentiality of photography. What he draws from the photograph of his mother aged five is a new definition of the punctum: no longer concerned with the 'detail', the punctum now refers to 'Time, the lacerating emphasis of the *noeme* ("*that-has-been*"), its pure representation' (CL: 95). Barthes argues that the paradox of photography, that renowned modern medium by which we apparently capture life and the living, lies in the fact that its punctum and true essence is to attest to the reality of death, the '*that-has-been*' of its referent. In *Empire of Signs*, among the many photographs included, Barthes had reproduced two photographs relevant to this point: General Nogi and his wife (the referent of the two photographs), having learnt of the death of the emperor, decided in September 1912 to commit suicide. They also decided to have their pictures taken on the day before their suicide. The two photographs capture perfectly what Barthes means by his new definition of the punctum: the photographs display the '*having-been-there*' of two people who have died but who, in the picture, *are going to die*. This is, according to Barthes, what all photographs do, presenting the presence, the reality, of the referent, at the same moment as asserting its pastness. The photographic referent, therefore, presents us with the reality of something which is in the past, and is therefore lost. Photographs, therefore, do not provide a direct analogy between an image and a referent; rather, they testify to the reality of that which has died or is going to die. Instead of providing a transparent, uncoded medium between image and reality, photographs disturb our habitual understanding of space and time. Barthes writes:

> the photograph's immobility is somehow the result of a perverse confusion
> between two concepts: the Real and the Live: by attesting that the object has

been real, the photograph surreptitiously induces belief that it is alive, because of that delusion which makes us attribute to Reality an absolutely superior, somehow eternal value; but by shifting this reality to the past ('*this-has-been*'), the photograph suggests that it is already dead.

(CL: 79)

In the climactic section in which Barthes recounts his discovery of the Winter Garden Photograph he writes of the experience of this feature of photography in terms of a double loss. In finding the photograph of his mother as a child, he writes:

I was then losing her twice over, in her final fatigue and in her first photograph, for me the last; but it was also at this moment that everything turned around and I discovered her *as into herself* . . .

(CL: 71)

In various descriptions of the new definition of the photographic punctum Barthes repeats this doubling effect: a process in which what is lost is found again only to be lost again:

What *pricks* me is the discovery of this equivalence. In front of the photograph of my mother as a child, I tell myself: she is going to die. I shudder . . . *over a catastrophe which has already occurred*. Whether or not the subject is already dead, every photograph is this catastrophe.

(CL: 96)

The pattern of losing the loved one, only to find them again in a photograph which necessarily repeats the experience of loss, is figured by Barthes as the 'moment' in which 'everything turns around'. This pattern is, in fact, what we have noted throughout this analysis of *Camera Lucida*: the initial theory of the distinction between studium and punctum breaking down in the first part of the book; Barthes, in the second part, resurrects that theoretical distinction upon a basis – the photograph of his mother and his personal response to it – which can only once again disqualify it as a general theory. The pattern, once we understand it as functioning as an emblem for the whole text, explains the paradox of *Camera Lucida*. Far from presenting a general theory of photography, Barthes's text brilliantly captures the impossibility of committing to language (the generalized sign-system of writing) a personal, emotional response which he, in defiance of language's generalizing violence, wishes to honour and express. Barthes's last book is a stunning act of defiance, a text which defies (writes in spite of) the knowledge of its own impossibility. It is a text written against the force with which he had struggled all his writing life: language's power to assimilate the new and the particular into that which is culturally accepted, generalized and thus disembodied. *Camera Lucida* strives to defend the image of his mother from acculturation (the generalizing violence of language), knowing that such a defence is impossible. It is a text written from Barthes's own body and, perhaps of all his numerous works, expresses most vividly and profoundly the unmistakable grain of his uniquely rebellious voice.

SUMMARY

In this chapter we have read Barthes's last book in the context of his later writing, registering within such a personal text an attempt to resist the solidifying violence inherent in all language. In *Camera Lucida* Barthes mixes theoretical writing with intense mourning for his mother in order to present a text which exemplifies what is unrepeatable in his later writing. Barthes's *Camera Lucida*, in pursuing an 'impossible' practice of writing (theoretical and yet personal, generalizing and yet purely individual) attempts to resist and defy the violence of language, which would turn his own mother into an archetype of *the* Mother. In performing such a personal act of writing, *Camera Lucida* offers to its readers many illuminating, if not immediately usable, insights into the nature of photography and representation generally.

AFTER BARTHES

When we speak of the influence of writers we tend to make the mistake of producing quantitative evaluations, as if influence were a singular thing of which a writer can have a lot or a little. One of the influences of Barthes's work should be that it makes us reconsider commonplace figures, such as the figure of influence. There are, after all, many kinds of influence. One way of registering this fact is to consider what we mean by a phrase such as 'after Barthes'. The word 'after' has a number of literary resonances. We might think of the 'after-piece' popular in the theatrical world between the eighteenth and nineteenth centuries. An after-piece was a play, frequently of a comical or farcical nature, usually of only one act, which was presented after the main production. We might also think of the tradition of writing poems in the style of or 'after' a great master, such as poems 'after Shakespeare' or 'after John Keats'. We need also, of course, to consider the word in its literal sense. If we consult a dictionary, we find that the word has conflicting meanings: that which is 'behind in place or order' (OED), for example, someone who is behind (after) the winner of a race; but also, that which is 'later in time, next following', or, in other words, someone or something which succeeds (comes after) someone or something else. The word 'after', it would appear, can mean being behind or it can mean being in front.

The first sense of the word 'after' we have located directs us to the event of and the immediate impact of Barthes's death, an event that in many ways was played out as a small, even farcical after-piece to Barthes's life. The second sense directs us to the more traditional meanings of the word 'influence', in particular to the question of whether Barthes's work has provided material for subsequent theorists and critics to imitate and emulate. The last sense of the word 'after' involves us in the more complex patterns of the influences of Barthes's work, including not only what elements of Barthes's work have been superseded and moved beyond, but also what elements still remain or even have yet to be realized.

THE DEATH OF ROLAND BARTHES

On 25 February 1980 Barthes attended a lunch party given by the future President of France, François Mitterrand. This kind of invitation certainly indicates the fame that Barthes had attained in his later life: Mitterrand is reported to have particularly enjoyed the descriptions of everyday French cultural life in *Mythologies* (see Calvet 1994: 248). On leaving the lunch party Barthes decided to walk home, but on stepping out to cross the Rue des Écoles he was hit by a passing laundry van. As Calvet puts it:

> Unconcious and bleeding from the nose, without his identity card or any other form of identification, he was taken to the Salpêtrière hospital by ambulance. No one knew who he was, which is why the media did not get hold of the news until much later.
>
> (Calvet 1994: 248)

Barthes lingered in hospital for almost exactly a month, visited by his friends and colleagues, before he died on 26 March. To many of those visitors it appeared that Barthes, never having recovered from his mother's death, simply lacked sufficient will to recover from his accident. It has been noted that within *Camera Lucida*, which had recently been published, Barthes refers to his text as 'my last investigation' (Todorov 2000: 128). Indeed, contemplating the Winter Garden Photograph and the implications of his mother's death, Barthes writes: 'Once she was dead I no longer had any reason to attune myself to the progress of the superior Life Force (the race, the species). . . . From now on I could do no more than await my total, undialectical death'

(CL: 72). Barthes's death, farcical as the laundry-van accident may seem, was tragically prepared by a death which preceded it. Barthes's death was also to be overshadowed by a death which, from the point of view of public notice, quickly overtook it. On 15 April 1980 Jean-Paul Sartre died. As Calvet writes:

> Barthes's funeral in the cemetery at Urt had been attended by a mere hand-ful of his friends, but Sartre's funeral in Montparnasse was to attract a crowd of over fifty thousand people. Moreover, the tenth anniversary of Barthes's death in 1990 was hardly given a mention in the media, whereas the anniversary of Sartre's death was marked by tributes to him on both radio and television.
>
> (Calvet 1994: 254)

The ironies involved in Sartre's death, hot on the heels of Barthes's own, involve issues of media coverage and the manner in which intellectuals are divided into 'famous' and 'less-than-famous' which immediately make one wish that Barthes had been alive to demythologize them. We would make a mistake, however, to read Calvet's account too literally and turn Barthes's death into a tragi-comic afterpiece in which the waters of history (in the shape of Sartre and national mourning for his demise) immediately swallowed whole his image and influence. Barthes had, and continues to have, a complex and ongoing influence which it is as important to understand today as it was in 1980 or 1990.

THE INFLUENCE OF ROLAND BARTHES

The influence of Barthes's ideas has had an immense impact on many different fields within the Humanities. No one writing today, for example, can discuss issues of literary authorship, still a hotly contested issue, without referring to Barthes's work on 'the death of the author'. Concepts such as the text and intertextuality continue to have a major impact on literary studies and are indelibly marked by Barthes's seminal work on these issues. The modern discipline and practice of cultural studies is shot through with the influence of Barthes and, in its contemporary form, can be said to draw a great deal of its rationale from texts such as *Mythologies*, *The Fashion System* and numerous essays ranging throughout Barthes's career as a theorist. No student engaged in a course on the media, or forms of representation, or politics and culture can afford to proceed in ignorance of Barthes's work.

Theoretical discussions of photography still rely heavily on Barthes's path-breaking work in this field; sections of the modern discipline of linguistics are still influenced by his work. New fields of theoretical and critical work, particularly those involved with the new information technologies and computer-systems in general, draw extensively from the work of Barthes. A pioneer in the fields of hypertextual theory and practice, George P. Landow gives a primary place to Barthes in his work, as do other leading theorists in this area (see Landow 1992, Landow 1994 and Tuman 1992). As scholars and critics explore the ways in which computer technologies allow us to reassess and develop our understanding of language and literature, Barthes's work on textuality and the reversibility of writerly texts continues to be one of the most profitable models upon which to base such research.

Barthes's work is, then, inextricably linked to the notion and practice of theory. When we engage in theoretical work of whatever kind, we practise a mode or modes of discourse which Barthes helped to establish. References to and citations of Barthes's work still abound in the various branches of what we nowadays call theoretical writing. Yet it remains true to say that no one practises theory *after* Barthes. For Tzvetan Todorov, Barthes is precisely not a 'master' who can be emulated, imitated, followed methodically. Todorov states that 'if there exist Barthesians somewhere in the world they do not find their shared identity in a stock of common concepts'. Barthes, Todorov argues, 'created a role for himself which consisted in subverting the mastery inherent in discourse, and in assuming that role he . . . made himself irreplaceable' (Todorov 2000: 123–4). Julia Kristeva, looking back on Barthes's work and its influence, supports Todorov's point that Barthes is not a master to be imitated but an irreplaceable writer: 'there are no Barthes "disciples," only epigones, as is often the case with writers' (Kristeva 2000: 140).

Readers of this work are in a position to appreciate why Barthes is not a theorist others can strictly imitate. Those who wish to follow Barthes's structuralist work on narrative must be aware of the manner in which he came to unravel such a procedure through the development of textual analysis. Those who would follow Barthes's demythologizing practice in books such as *Mythologies* must be aware that, in his later work, Barthes came to radically question such a method, on both a theoretical and an ideological level. Those who would emulate Barthes's later, hedonistic style of criticism cannot avoid the fact that such an approach is by definition beyond the realms of a social and intellectual community, beyond, that is, anything which is shareable and thus open to imitation and emulation. One cannot write *after* a hedonist.

Barthes, as we have seen, was committed throughout his writing career to discourses that were new or at least resisted easy categorization. Throughout his life Barthes put his voice behind discourses which had not, as yet, been acculturated by dominant ideology. What this means for his own legacy as a thinker and writer is that numerous concepts, promising beginnings or essays, a host of one-off methods and approaches, await those who come after him. None of these elements, however, amount to a stable and permanent method since, as we have seen throughout this study, Barthes did not believe in the possibility of a method that could avoid assimilation by dominant culture. Barthes's work, then, forces us to question what we mean by the word 'theory'. Is theory a methodology by which we systematically analyse literary and cultural texts? Or is theory a disruptive force which questions all available methods but never offers a definite method in their place? Is theory a positive force within the disciplines which make up the Humanities (literary studies, cultural studies, history, sociology, linguistics, philosophy and so on)? Or is theory an essentially negative force which disturbs and displaces the methodologies by which the various disciplines within the Humanities would define themselves? Barthes's influence is so diffuse and so difficult to categorize precisely because he comes down so firmly on the side of the second of these two options for theory.

Barthes's work asks us to follow after him by finding new critical objects of study and new critical approaches rather than attempting the impossible task of imitating his methods and his modes of writing. Barthes's various methods, it is also true to say, remain available for us to use in a limited, localized or strategic manner, picking them up for a particular task but always with a full sense of the temporary nature of such an exercise. We cannot rely on Barthes for a method, as some psychoanalysts still rely on Freud, or as most physicists still rely on Einstein. It is, in fact, impossible to imitate Barthes, since the question of which 'Barthes' we are imitating among the many 'Barthes' which are available disrupts the very notion of the imitation of an author.

To write *after* Barthes is, paradoxical as it may seem, to avoid imitating him. One need only remember the argument of 'The Death of the Author' and the critique of the 'myth of filiation' which surrounds the figure of the author to register the appropriateness of such an apparent paradox. The author of 'The Death of the Author' should not and perhaps cannot be reduced, by those who come after him, to 'the author of structuralism' or 'the author of textual analysis'. Barthes studiously avoided becoming an 'author' (a 'master') in this sense: for him, writing did not lead to the establishment of a movement or a school of thought; writing, for Barthes, as he once famously put it, is an intransitive verb, a verb which does not need an Object to complete its action (RL: 11–21). The meaning of writing, in other words, lies within the activity of writing itself rather than in what one is supposed to produce by that activity. Writing, for Barthes, *is* a meaning or, perhaps, a disturbance of meaning rather than a production *of* a meaning.

THE INFLUENCES OF BARTHES

The last twenty years have been characterized by concerns, theoretical debates, and general social and cultural transformations which were only beginning to exist when Barthes died in 1980. Feminist theory, the dominant theoretical mode of debate in this period, has often taken important ideas and theoretical examples from Barthes, but it has done so through a creative rereading of Barthes's work which directs that work towards issues which were not its original, primary focus (see, for example, Nancy K. Miller 1988). D.A. Miller's 'outing' of Barthes as a homosexual writer in his *Bringing Out Roland Barthes* (1992) performs a similar function for 'queer theory'. Yet, we might ask, what has Barthes got to tell us about the most pressing and compelling issues of our current moment of history? If our history is currently dominated by questions of globalization, rhetorical and yet at the same time tragically real wars against 'terrorism', the rise of nationalisms uncon-nected to existing nation states, issues revolving around the relation between human and artificial intelligence, the human body and the technological body, the relation between 'hard' reality and the world of the web, then does Barthes's work still have relevance besides the flashes of illumination and brilliant suggestiveness it clearly continues to offer? Barthes's work is centred squarely in a post-war, French context and revolves around the antagonism between the avant-garde in art and in thought and a bourgeoisie which Barthes from first to last saw as the dominant force in his society and culture. As Colin MacCabe puts it:

> From one perspective it is foolish to assess Barthes's importance . . . after his death. Barthes cannot participate in the debates and circumstances of the 1990s [or the 2000s]. He will remain forever part of the period from the Liberation to the end of the Cold War – his texts simply do not reflect the final failure of Soviet planning, the perceived collapse of World War II political settlements, or the renewed importance of nationalism . . . he appears caught up in yesterday's arguments and priorities; whatever the elegance of his writing (which is always considerable) his texts often seem very dated.
>
> (MacCabe 1997: 72)

The world we live in now, in other words, is very different from the world Barthes was born into and in which he lived. Barthes died only two decades ago, yet the world map and the issues which preoccupy us have altered drastically in that time.

One has to be careful when suggesting that Barthes's relevance and thus potential influence has died, however. In fact, such a statement would only really make sense if it was directed towards a theorist who presented a method which was meant to be relevant in all possible contexts. For such a theorist and for such a method, altered conditions in society and culture can prove fatal. Barthes, however, studiously avoided all such claims to general significance. In his 'The Deaths of Roland Barthes', Jacques Derrida asks: 'didn't he [Barthes] himself speak right up until the very last moment about his death and, metonymically, about his deaths?' (Derrida 2001: 59). This is a telling question which illuminates many passages within Barthes's work which might otherwise remain unconsidered. Certainly, at the very moment in which he is introducing his book *The Fashion System* Barthes tells his readers that the method displayed so rigorously within that text is already superseded in relevance, the method he states 'is already dated' (FS: ix) and, we might add, 'dead'. We have also seen how in later essays, such as 'The Image' of 1978, Barthes associates all names and all processes of giving stable and fixed names to people and to forms of writing with a kind of death. He writes there, as elsewhere, of the various ways in which he himself as a writer has been turned into an 'image'. The image here is a kind of death, a false covering, a stereotype which smothers writing in a rigid appearance of meaning. In his essay 'Writers, Intellectuals, Teacher', Barthes states that 'we may call a "writer" (this word always designating a practice, not a social value) any sender whose "message" (thereby immediately destroying its nature as message) cannot be summarized' (RL: 312). Death, in Barthes's work, seems to be analogous to the process of assimilation he strove so hard to resist all his writing life. For Barthes, to die is to be assimilated into a name, an image, a meaning, to find one's writing transformed into a singular, stable and communicable (summarizable) meaning. We can extend this point by recognizing that the ultimate 'death' for Barthes would have been to have generated a theoretical method slavishly followed (imitated) by 'disciples' writing *after* him.

Barthes presents his readers less with an influence than with an example. This example involves a practice rather than a fixed set of ideas or methodological procedures: the practice of a mode of writing which is committed to the expression of that which is not as yet assimilated, which is not yet part of an academic or a general cultural consensus. To be influenced by Barthes is to be affected by an example of a writing practice which is inimitable and yet which, in all its myriad forms, demonstrates the continued possibility of a mode of commitment. What that commitment involves has been the subject of this entire study and can only be summarized through recourse to the name (a signifier with no ultimate signified) of Roland Barthes. The influence of Roland Barthes can be felt by his readers whenever a theorist or a novelist, a philosopher or a photographer, a student in an essay or a designer of an advertisement campaign, does something with the available language which is not expected or not supposed to happen. The example of Barthes is not only something that speaks to us from his works, and thus from the past, but something we should aspire to become in the future.

FURTHER READING

WORKS BY ROLAND BARTHES

Barthes's complete works are available in *Œuvres complètes*, three vols, ed. Eric Marty, Paris: Le Seuil, 1993–5.

—— (1953) *Le Degré zéro de l'écriture*, Paris: Le Seuil. (English version, *Writing Degree Zero*, trans. Annette Lavers and Colin Smith, London: Jonathan Cape, 1984.)

Barthes's first major work. A response to Sartre's *What is Literature?*, among other influences, the book redirects Marxist and Existentialist theories of literature and commitment to the issue of language, style and writing (écriture). Presenting both a theory of the three terms just mentioned, along with a history of French literature since the eighteenth century, Barthes at once champions the writing of such contemporaries as Albert Camus, at the same time as arguing that no form of writing can ultimately resist absorption by and into bourgeois culture ('Literature'). Also available as *Writing Degree Zero*, trans. Annette Lavers and Colin Smith (New York: Hill and Wang, 2001), this edition contains the important 1968 Preface by Susan Sontag.

—— (1954) *Michelet par lui-même*, Paris: Le Seuil. (English version, *Michelet*, trans. Richard Howard, New York: Hill and Wang, 1987.)

Barthes's reading of the nineteenth-century French historian Michelet. Combines various theoretical approaches, including linguistic, historical and psychoanalytic criticism, to read Michelet, but also follows the concern of the series within which the book was published to read its author *par lui-même* ('by and for himself') by including extensive extracts from Michelet's own writing.

—— (1957) *Mythologies*, Paris: Le Seuil. (English version, *Mythologies*, trans. Annette Lavers, London: Jonathan Cape, 1972; *The Eiffel Tower and Other Mythologies*, trans. Richard Howard, New York: Hill and Wang, 1979.)

Barthes's *Mythologies* originate in a series of essays written, one a month, between 1954 and 1956 and published mainly in *Les Lettres Nouvelles*. All the essays, with the exception of 'Astrologie', have been collected in two English language collections, *Mythologies* and *The Eiffel Tower*, with the addition of five essays not originally included in the French: 'The Two Salons', 'Dining Car', 'Cottage Industry', 'Buffet Finishes Off New York', and 'The Eiffel Tower' (all included in Barthes, *The Eiffel Tower*, 1979). Barthes's *Mythologies* is one of his most widely read and influential books. It represents a sustained, at times extremely witty and satirical, attempt to demonstrate the ability of semiology to read the numerous 'myths' which make up contemporary (in this case French) culture.

—— (1963) *Sur Racine*, Paris: Le Seuil. (English version, *On Racine*, trans. Richard Howard, New York: Hill and Wang, 1964.)

On Racine, along with an 'Introduction' situating the book in the context of contemporary critical approaches, collects three essays on the canonical French playwright. The first and largest essay, 'Racinian Man', employs structuralist and psychoanalytical approaches to analyse the fundamental elements of Racinian tragic drama. The second essay, 'Racine Spoken', focuses on the modern bourgeois theatre's tendency to familiarize Racinian tragic drama, giving undue weight to the performance of actors and actresses and to a certain form of delivery which takes meaning from the 'details' emphasized, rather than from the formal meaning of Racine's alexandrine lines of poetry. The 'music' of Racine, in other words, is, in modern bourgeois theatre, thought to depend on the delivery of actors and actresses, rather than on Racine's highly formalized and historically distanced poetry. The third essay, 'History or Literature', attacks what Barthes calls 'university criticism' and argues for its replacement by explicitly theoretical approaches to literature.

—— (1964) *Essais critiques*, Paris: Le Seuil. (English version, *Critical Essays*, trans. Richard Howard, Evanston: Northwestern University Press, 1972.)

Of all the collections of his essays published during and after his lifetime, *Critical Essays* is perhaps the most important. A major expression of Barthes's work up to the mid-1960s, the collection contains essays which complement his work on 'literature', 'writing' and 'commitment', his work on Brechtian and bourgeois theatre, on the nouveau roman, on the avant-garde and on modern 'myths'. The collection also includes important essays in which the emergence of semiology and structuralism is registered.

—— (1964) *Eléments de sémiologie*, *Communications*, no. 4, republished as *Le Degré zéro de l'ecriture, suive de: Eléments de sémiologie*, Paris: Gonthier, 1965. (English version, published with *Writing Degree Zero*, *Elements of Semiology*, trans. Annette Lavers and Colin Smith, London: Jonathan Cape, 1984.)

Elements of Semiology is Barthes's most sustained attempt to lay the theoretical foundations for the kind of semiological work to be found in *Mythologies*, *The Fashion System* and related work of this period.

—— (1966) *Critique et verité*, Paris: Le Seuil. (English version, *Criticism and Truth*, trans. Katrine Pilcher Keuneman, London: The Athlone Press, 1987.)

Criticism and Truth is Barthes's response to Raymond Picard's *New Criticism or New Fraud?* and the many other articles and press pieces which supported Picard's critique of the 'new criticism'. The book is divided into two parts. Part One answers Picard and his followers directly. Part Two presents an analysis of what it means for criticism to concern itself with language.

—— (1967) *Système de la mode*, Paris: Le Seuil. (English version, *The Fashion System*, trans. Matthew Ward and Richard Howard, New York: Hill and Wang, 1983.)

Barthes researched and wrote the bulk of this study between 1957 and 1963. The study begins with a Foreword, written at the time of publication in 1967, which already shows Barthes moving away from this kind of semiology towards a more post-structuralist understanding of the sign. The study is offered to Barthes's readers, therefore, as a moment in the 'history of semiology' (p. ix). The text itself presents

Barthes's most sustained engagement with semiology conceived as a scientific reading of cultural sign systems.

—— (1970) *L'Empire des signes*, Geneva: Skira. (English version, *Empire of Signs*, trans. Richard Howard, New York: Hill and Wang, 1982.)

Barthes's study of Japan is not meant as an accurate reflection of Japanese culture. Barthes wrote his book while many of his *Tel Quel* colleagues were championing the Marxist regime in neighbouring China. The text is, then, intentionally controversial and is meant less as an actual description than as a productive response to the material signs of an alien (Other) culture. There is no mention in Barthes's text of the phenomenon of Japanese post-war capitalism. Rather, Japan is read as a text against and within which Barthes can explore the emergent post-structuralist and deconstructive theories which were beginning to radically influence and transform his work as a writer.

—— (1970) *S/Z*, Paris: Le Seuil. (English version, *S/Z*, trans. Richard Miller, New York: Hill and Wang, 1974.)

S/Z is undoubtedly Barthes's most important single reading of a literary text. Taking a short story by Balzac, *Sarrasine*, Barthes produces over two hundred pages of commentary and analysis, testifying thereby to the radical plurality of literary texts. *S/Z* is usually seen as the text which embodies the movement away from structuralist literary criticism (particularly the structural analysis of narratives) towards post-structuralism.

—— (1971) *Sade, Fourier, Loyola*, Paris: Le Seuil. (English version, *Sade/Fourier/Loyola*, trans. Richard Miller, New York: Hill and Wang, 1976.)

This text brings together pieces written on the Marquis de Sade, Saint Ignatius of Loyola and Charles Fourier. The text is purposefully controversial in its choice of subject matter, since, to combine these three writers under one cover, is to mix the erotic (pornographic) writing of Sade with the spiritual writing of Ignatius, Father of the Jesuit order, along with the political utopianism of Fourier. Barthes's concern, however, is less with the content of these three authors than with similarities in their writing. All three authors, widely different as the 'message' of their texts may be, are 'logothetes', by which Barthes means that they are 'founders of a language'. Barthes's readings excel in highlighting each author's obsessive concern with systems and codes, categorizations and lists. His analyses demonstrate the manner in which each of these three authors are ultimately less interested in the relation between their texts and the world than with the coherence, logic and internal unity of their language. In this sense, each of these authors is shown by Barthes to produce writing, understanding that term in the context of Barthes's earlier works, such as *Writing Degree Zero*.

—— (1972) *Nouveaux essais critiques*, Paris: Le Seuil. (English version, *New Critical Essays*, trans. Richard Howard, New York: Hill and Wang, 1980.)

Originally published in French with a reprint of *Writing Degree Zero*, Barthes's *New Critical Essays* contains important pieces on La Rochefoucauld, 'The Plates of the *Encylopedia*', Chateaubriand's *Life of Rancé* and, perhaps most importantly, essays on 'Proust and Names' and 'Flaubert and the Sentence'.

—— (1973) *Le Plaisir du texte*, Paris: Le Seuil. (English version, *The Pleasure of the Text*, trans. Richard Miller, New York: Hill and Wang, 1975.)

Impossible to summarize, *The Pleasure of the Text* is Barthes's major expression of an erotic, hedonist model of reading; a model of reading which takes account, that is, of the bodily response of the reader towards the text. Divided into forty-six fragmentary sections, the text organizes itself by placing each section in alphabetical order according to the single word headings listed in the 'Contents' page but omitted in the main body of the text itself. *The Pleasure of the Text* is, then, a reversible text, resisting the development of a coherent, linear argument and establishing in its place a series of binary terms, most importantly between pleasure (plaisir) and bliss (jouissance). Readers should note that Miller consistently translates signifiance as 'signification', thus erasing from the English version some of the nuances involved in that former term.

—— (1975) *Roland Barthes*, Paris: Le Seuil. (English version, *Roland Barthes by Roland Barthes*, trans. Richard Howard, London: Macmillan, 1977.)

This text was written in the same series as Barthes's *Michelet*, the 'Écrivains de toujours' introductory series published by Le Seuil. The striking feature, of course, is the literal manner in which Barthes takes the rubric of the series, *par lui-même* ('by and for himself'). *Roland Barthes* is an unclassifiable text, lying somewhere between autobiography, theoretical critique of his own previous works and a fictionalized account of a figure referred to variously as 'RB', 'he' and in the first-person ('I' and 'me'). The text begins with the statement 'It must all be considered as if spoken by a character in a novel', thus alerting the reader to the instability both of the object of the text ('Roland Barthes') and the subjective voice writing the text ('Roland Barthes'). In many ways, then, *Roland Barthes* is a text which gives us a glimpse of what writing the self (autobiography) might look like after 'the death of the author'.

—— (1977) *Fragments d'un discours amoureux*, Paris: Le Seuil. (English version, *A Lover's Discourse: Fragments*, trans. Richard Howard, New York: Hill and Wang, 1978.)

Barthes's famous exploration of the discourse of the amorous subject (the lover) has always, since the moment of its publication, been one of his most popular and widely read texts. Divided into brief sections, arranged alphabetically, the text takes the reader through what some consider to be a novelistic journey covering the major intertextual figures which make up the Western discourse of love. The text is written by a subject who is at one and the same time Barthes himself, every reader and ultimately the 'I' (any 'I') which speaks the discourse of love. *A Lover's Discourse* in this sense encapsulates that blend of systematic and personalized writing which so characterizes Barthes's later style as a writer.

—— (1977) *Image-Music-Text*, selected and trans. Stephen Heath, London: Fontana/Collins.

This popular collection of essays has provided many English-speaking readers with their first introduction to Barthes's writing. Containing many of Barthes's seminal essays, the collection is now somewhat overshadowed by the publication of all of Barthes's major essay collections in English.

—— (1978) *Leçon*, Paris: Le Seuil. (English version, 'Inaugural Lecture, Collège de France' in *Barthes: Selected Writings*, ed. Susan Sontag, op. cit., 457–78.)

A major statement by Barthes of his approach to semiology (his chair was in 'Literary Semiology') but also to teaching; Barthes here is concerned, in particular, with the relationship between pedagogy and power.

―――― (1979) *Sollers Écrivain*, Paris: Le Seuil. (English version, *Sollers Writer*, trans. Philip Thody, London: The Athlone Press, 1987.)

This text collects together various essays written by Barthes on his friend and colleague, the avant-garde novelist Philippe Sollers. The most important of these six essays, originally published between 1965 and 1978, is entitled 'Drama, Poem, Novel' and deals with Sollers's text *Drame*. The main text of this essay was originally published in the journal *Critique* in 1965; the version included here contains a commentary by Barthes on the original essay. A different translation of the essay can be found at the end of the English version of Sollers's text, translated as *Event* by Bruce Benderson and Ursule Molinaro (see Sollers, 1986).

―――― (1980) *La Chambre claire: note sur la photographie*, Paris: Gallimard Le Seuil. (English version, *Camera Lucida: Reflections on Photography*, trans. Richard Howard, New York: Hill and Wang, 1981.)

Barthes's last book to be published during his lifetime. At once an analytical study of the nature of photography and a deeply personal meditation on the loss of his mother, this text continues to produce significant discussion and debate. The distinction between studium and punctum introduced in Barthes's 'note' on photography can usefully be read in terms of the dominant themes of Barthes's later work, marking the difference, as they do, between a general and socially communicable photographic meaning and a unique, unrepeatable and personal meaning registered on a bodily level. While some critics have suggested that Barthes's arguments here contradict the main thrust of his post-structuralist work, the text can also be read (as it is in this study) as a defiant and highly serious work wholly in tune with Barthes's post-structuralist views concerning the assimilative, even violent nature of language.

―――― (1981) *Le grain de la voix: entretiens 1962–1980*, Paris: Le Seuil. (English version, *The Grain of the Voice: Interviews 1962–1980*, trans. Linda Coverdale, New York: Hill and Wang, 1985.)

A crucial resource for anyone conducting research on Barthes. Collects a large, if not exhaustive, array of interviews from 1962 onwards. Barthes was a regular interviewee and his charm and wit are always evident in his responses and statements. The collection demonstrates the manner in which Barthes adapted himself to different discursive contexts: he did not, obviously, speak with the same critical and theoretical voice in interviews conducted by *Tel Quel*, *Les Lettres françaises*, *Le Monde*, *Le Figaro* and the European edition of *Playboy*.

—— (1982) *Barthes: Selected Writings*, ed. Susan Sontag, Oxford: Fontana.

A more extensive collection of texts and extracts than *Image-Music-Text*, this text has had a similar role in the dissemination of Barthes's key ideas within the English-speaking world. Contains an important introductory essay by the editor and continues to be a necessary text due to the inclusion of Barthes's 'Inaugural Lecture, Collège de France'.

—— (1982) *L'obvie et l'obtus*, Paris: Le Seuil. (English version, *The Responsibility of Forms: Critical Essays on Music, Arts, and Representation*, trans. Richard Howard, New York: Hill and Wang, 1985.)

A major collection of essays for those readers interested in Barthes's work on music and the visual arts. As with *The Semiotic Challenge*, readers of this text can place the well-known and frequently anthologized essays in a fuller and more progressive context.

—— (1984) *Le bruissement de la langue*, Paris: Le Seuil. (English version, *The Rustle of Language*, trans. Richard Howard, New York: Hill and Wang, 1986.)

A major collection of essays on a diverse range of subjects within the realms of literature, linguistics and theory. Contains seminal essays such as 'The Death of the Author' and 'From Work to Text', but places these essays by the side of less familiar but related essays. Translated by Richard Howard, the collection provides new translations of much quoted essays, thus serving to denaturalize what have become canonical versions in English. In this study, for example, I have quoted from Howard's translation of 'The Death of the Author' rather than from the more famous translation by Stephen Heath in *Image-Music-Text*.

—— (1985) *L'aventure sémiologique*, Paris: Le Seuil. (English version, *The Semiotic Challenge*, trans. Richard Howard, Oxford: Blackwell, 1988.)

A collection, published after Barthes's death, which assembles his major essays on narrative theory, along with important essays on semiology. The collection as a whole is an invaluable guide to the development of Barthes's thought during the structuralist phase of his career and, in particular, takes the reader through Barthes's engagement with the structural analysis of narratives to its transformation into what he calls 'textual analysis'. This is an indispensable text for any reader wishing to focus on the development of Barthes's approach to narrative fiction.

——— (1987) *Incidents*, Paris: Le Seuil. (English version, *Incidents*, trans. Richard Howard, Berkeley and Los Angeles: University of California Press, 1992.)

Posthumously published pieces by Barthes of an autobiographical nature. Of the four pieces included, 'The Light of the Sud-Ouest' and 'At Le Palace Tonight . . .' had been previously published in 1977 in *L'Humanité*. 'Incidents', a journal written by Barthes during his stay in Morocco between 1968 and 1969, and 'Soirées de Paris' ('Paris Evenings') written in 1979, had not previously been published. The sexually explicit nature of 'Incidents' and the rather personal account of friends and colleagues in 'Soirées de Paris' caused controversy when they were finally published. Whether these texts should have been published at all is a question posed by many commentators; however, as Diana Knight suggests, after their appearance it is difficult 'not to accept them as part of Barthes's *œuvre*' (Knight, 1997a: 17). Certainly, 'Incidents' and 'At Le Palace Tonight . . .' offer fascinating material for those interested in Barthes as a gay writer and thinker, while 'Soirées de Paris' contributes greatly to our sense of Barthes's isolation, fatigue and sense of loss in the last year of his life.

WORKS ON ROLAND BARTHES

BOOKS

Bensmaïa, Réda (1987) *The Barthes Effect: The Essay as Reflective Text*, trans. Pat Fedkiew, Minneapolis: University of Minnesota Press.

A study of Barthes which places his work within the ancient but generally overlooked tradition of essay writing. Barthes's use of the fragment, Bensmaïa argues, challenges dominant ideas about the genres of writing and links him to unclassifiable writers such as the sixteenth-century essayist Montaigne.

Brown, Andrew (1992) *Roland Barthes: The Figures of Writing*, Oxford: Clarendon Press.

A major contribution to the theories it describes and discusses, Brown's book is an original and complex engagement with Barthes as a writer. Treating Barthes not simply as a theorist of paraphraseable ideas but as a writer, Brown organizes his study through various 'figures of writing' which are observable within Barthes's work: drifting, frames and names, scribbling and trauma.

Calvet, Louis-Jean (1994) *Roland Barthes*, trans. Sarah Wykes, Oxford: Polity Press.

An enjoyable, informative and illuminating biography of Barthes's life. Places Barthes within his social and cultural milieu. Calvet discusses Barthes's texts, but this is fundamentally a biography rather than a work of criticism.

Champagne, Roland (1984) *Literary History in the Wake of Roland Barthes: Redefining the Myths of Reading*, Birmingham, Alabama: Summa Publications.

Champagne is concerned to demonstrate ways in which Barthes's work has major implications for the manner in which we think of and practise literary history.

Culler, Jonathan (2002) *Roland Barthes: A Very Short Introduction*, Oxford: Oxford University Press.

Originally published in 1983 in the Fontana Modern Masters series and now republished in OUP's *A Very Short Introduction* series, this is still an excellent guide to Barthes's basic ideas and can be read very profitably alongside the current text.

Freedman, Sanford and Carole Anne Taylor (1983) *Roland Barthes: A Bibliographical Reader's Guide*, New York and London: Garland.

An indispensable bibliographical guide for advanced study of Barthes. The guide contains very useful summaries of texts and thus is also of great use for less advanced readers. Only of use, of course, up to the early 1980s and thus readers must go elsewhere for information on the texts by and on Barthes published after this date.

Knight, Diana (1997) *Barthes and Utopia: Space, Travel, Writing*, Oxford: Clarendon Press.

One of the best studies yet written about Barthes. Knight takes the figure of utopia as a guiding element in Barthes's work and demonstrates the many ways in which it can provide fresh perspectives on both the most well-known texts and the lesser known articles and essays. Knight's book is immensely informative about all aspects of Barthes's work.

Knight, Diana (ed.) (2000) *Critical Essays on Roland Barthes*, New York: G. K. Hall.

A major collection of essays on Barthes. The collection is usefully divided into chronological periods: 'French Reception: Early Reviews (1953–1958)'; 'French Reception: The Heyday (1965–1980)'; 'French Reception: Barthes Remembered (1980–1984)'. Other sections compile major responses to Barthes by Anglo-American critics and theorists.

Lavers, Annette (1982) *Roland Barthes: Structuralism and After*, London: Methuen.

One of the earliest and best book-length studies of Barthes. Still cited by today's scholars and commentators, the book is something of a landmark in the critical and theoretical reception of Barthes's work.

Lombardo, Patrizia (1989) *The Three Paradoxes of Roland Barthes*, Athens and London: The University of Georgia Press.

A sophisticated and deeply engaged analysis of Barthes which is organized around a favourite Barthesian term: paradox. Divided into three chapters, the study presents an analysis of Barthes in terms of various productive paradoxes.

McGraw, Betty R. and Steven Ungar (eds) (1989) *Signs in Culture: Roland Barthes Today*, Iowa: University of Iowa Press.

A useful collection of essays on Barthes, including essays by Richard Howard, Antoine Compagnon, Mary Lydon and Steven Ungar.

Miller, D. A. (1992) *Bringing Out Roland Barthes*, Berkeley: University of California Press.

Miller's text is an important intervention on the question of Barthes's critical and theoretical voice and presence as a gay man. Written in a way which at once captures and yet radically departs from Barthes's own, writerly voice, Miller's text is a provocation to all of Barthes's readers who would miss, willfully or not, the challenge of his homosexuality and its inscription in his work.

Moriarty, Michael (1991) *Roland Barthes*, Oxford: Polity Press.

An essential study for all readers of Barthes. Manages the difficult task of combining clear introductions to the major works with significant theoretical interventions on the political, cultural and literary implications of Barthes's writing.

Mortimer, Armine Kotin (1989) *The Gentlest Law: Roland Barthes's 'The Pleasure of the Text'*, New York: Peter Lang.

A painstaking guide to *The Pleasure of the Text*, providing commentary and intertextual annotations for each section of Barthes's text. Particularly useful on issues of translation, intertexts and the intellectual context of Barthes's text.

Rabaté, Jean-Michel (ed.) (1997) *Writing the Image After Roland Barthes*, Philadelphia: University of Pennsylvania Press.

An essential collection of essays for anyone interested in Barthes's influence on the theory and criticism of the visual arts and photography in particular. The collection contains a host of essays by significant authors in the field and is a testament to the importance of this aspect of Barthes's writing. The collection also includes important essays on Barthes and literary topics.

Ribière, Mireille (2002) *Barthes: A Beginner's Guide*, London: Hodder & Stoughton.

A useful enough guide for those who want quick access to some of the major theoretical and critical aspects of Barthes's work.

Rylance, Rick (1994) *Roland Barthes*, Modern Critical Theorists, Hemel Hempstead: Harvester Wheatsheaf.

Published in the Modern Critical Theorists series, this study is an excellent introductory account of Barthes's entire work and can usefully be read alongside the current study. Rylance's use of a distinction between Barthes 'hot' and 'cold' provides a neat method for distinguishing between the more systematic and ludic (playful) tendencies within Barthes's work.

Shawcross, Nancy M. (1997) *Roland Barthes on Photography: The Critical Tradition in Perspective*, Gainsville: University Press of Florida.

This study is an immensely useful one for anyone wishing to learn more about Barthes's work on photography. Particularly useful for its discussion of the history of photography, Shawcross's text explains clearly and coherently the choices Barthes makes in the development of his account of the photographic image.

Stafford, Andy (1998) *Roland Barthes, Phenomenon and Myth: An Intellectual Biography*, Edinburgh: Edinburgh University Press.

This book returns Barthes's essays and major texts to their specific cultural moments. The effect is to produce a very different narrative to the one usually given of Barthes's career: a kind of month-by-month account which reads Barthes from the origins of his ideas through to their ends.

Thody, Philip (1977) *Roland Barthes: A Conservative Estimate*, London: Macmillan.

As the subtitle suggests, this is a sceptical appreciation of Barthes's work. Thody is particularly good at noting similarities and differences between Barthes's work and ideas, and approaches within the British critical and literary tradition. Since his preferences seem to be with what he sees as the more empirical British tradition, it is not always clear whether Thody wishes us to embrace or reject Barthes's work.

Ungar, Steven (1983) *Roland Barthes: The Professor of Desire*, Lincoln and London: University of Nebraska Press.

An illuminating and exceptionally lucid study of Barthes's œuvre. Ungar rightfully includes extensive discussions of Barthes's approach to teaching within his account of the movement from structuralism to post-structuralism. Barthes's move away from a science of literature towards 'figuration' in his later writings is read, by Ungar, in terms of a profession of desire and the bodily basis of reading which has important implications for pedagogy as well as for criticism.

Wiseman, Mary Bittner (1989) *The Ecstasies of Roland Barthes*, London: Routledge.

An imaginative and philosophical response, particularly to Barthes's later work, Wiseman's book possesses many challenges and provocations for seasoned readers and researchers of Barthes's work, but is in no sense an introduction.

BARTHES ONLINE

There is a useful selection of entries on Barthes in the *Semiotics* site at the University of Colorado at Denver; this includes a link to Sarah

Zupko's Cultural Studies Centre or *PopCultures.com* which contains scholarly articles, biographical pieces and selections from Barthes's work. George P. Landow's *Roland Barthes and the Writerly Text* produces a hypertext version of pages from his book *Hypertext*, along with additional materials of interest. Robert Clark's *Literary Encyclopedia and Literary Dictionary* has a number of entries on Barthes by the author of this study; these include longer accounts of some texts by Barthes than are included here, and thus offer readers the chance to extend their knowledge of Barthes's key ideas.

WORKS CITED

Adorno, Theodor (1991) *The Culture Industry: Selected Essays on Mass Culture*, ed. and intro. J.M. Bernstein, London and New York: Routledge.

Allen, Graham (2000) *Intertextuality*, The New Critical Idiom, London: Routledge.

Attridge, Derek (1997) 'Roland Barthes's Obtuse, Sharp Meaning and the Responsibilities of Commentary', in Jean-Michael Rabaté (ed.) *Writing the Image After Roland Barthes*, Philadelphia: University of Pennsylvania Press, 77–89.

Bakhtin, Mikhail (1984) *Problems of Dostoevsky's Poetics*, trans. and ed. C. Emerson, Minneapolis: University of Minnesota Press.

—— (1986) *Speech Genres and Other Late Essays*, trans. V.W. McGee, eds C. Emerson and M. Holquist, Austin, Tex.: University of Texas Press.

—— and V.N. Volosinov (1986) *Marxism and the Philosophy of Language*, trans. L. Matejka and I.R. Titunik, Cambridge, Mass. and London: Harvard University Press.

Barthes, Roland (1964) *On Racine*, trans. Richard Howard, New York: Hill and Wang.

—— (1972) *Critical Essays*, trans. Richard Howard, Evanston: Northwestern University Press.

—— (1972) *Mythologies*, trans. Annette Lavers, London: Jonathan Cape.

—— (1974) *S/Z*, trans. Richard Miller, New York: Hill and Wang.

—— (1975) *The Pleasure of the Text*, trans. Richard Miller, New York: Hill and Wang.

—— (1976) *Sade, Fourier, Loyola*, trans. Richard Miller, New York: Hill and Wang.

—— (1977) *Roland Barthes by Roland Barthes*, trans. Richard Howard, London: Macmillan.

—— (1977) *Image-Music-Text*, selected and trans. Stephen Heath, London: Fontana/Collins.

—— (1978) *A Lover's Discourse: Fragments*, trans. Richard Howard, New York: Hill and Wang.

—— (1979) *The Eiffel Tower and Other Mythologies*, trans. Richard Howard, New York: Hill and Wang.

—— (1980) *New Critical Essays*, trans. Richard Howard, New York: Hill and Wang.

—— (1981) 'Theory of the Text' in Robert Young (ed.) *Untying the Text: A Post-Structuralist Reader*, trans. Ian McLeod, London: Routledge and Kegan Paul, 31–47.

—— (1981) *Camera Lucida: Reflections on Photography*, trans. Richard Howard, New York: Hill and Wang.

—— (1982) *Empire of Signs*, trans. Richard Howard, New York: Hill and Wang.

—— (1982) *Barthes: Selected Writings*, ed. Susan Sontag, Oxford: Fontana.

—— (1983) *The Fashion System*, trans. Matthew Ward and Richard Howard, New York: Hill and Wang.

—— (1984) *Writing Degree Zero*, trans. Annette Lavers and Colin Smith, London: Jonathan Cape.

—— (1984) *Elements of Semiology*, trans. Annette Lavers and Colin Smith, London: Jonathan Cape.

—— (1985) *The Grain of the Voice: Interviews 1962–1980*, trans. Linda Coverdale, New York: Hill and Wang.

—— (1985) *The Responsibility of Forms: Critical Essays on Music, Art, and Representation*, trans. Richard Howard, New York: Hill and Wang.

—— (1986) 'Event, Poem, Novel' in Philippe Sollers, *Event*, trans. Bruce Benderson and Ursule Molinaro, New York: Red Dust.

—— (1986) *The Rustle of Language*, trans. Richard Howard, New York: Hill and Wang.

—— (1987) *Sollers Writer*, trans. Philip Thody, London: The Athlone Press.

—— (1987) *Michelet*, trans. Richard Howard, New York: Hill and Wang.

—— (1987) *Criticism and Truth*, trans. Katrine Pilcher Keuneman, London: The Athlone Press.

—— (1988) *The Semiotic Challenge*, trans. Richard Howard, Oxford: Blackwell.

—— (1993–5) *Œuvres complètes*, three vols., ed. Eric Marty, Paris: Le Seuil.

—— (1998) 'Responses: Interview with *Tel Quel*' in Patrick ffrench and Roland-François Lack (eds) *The 'Tel Quel' Reader*, trans. Vérène Grieshaber, London and New York: Routledge.

—— (2001) *Writing Degree Zero*, trans. Annette Lavers and Colin Smith, Preface by Susan Sontag, New York: Hill and Wang.

Bensmaïa, Réda (1987) *The Barthes Effect: The Essay as Reflective Text*, trans. Pat Fedkiew, Minneapolis: University of Minnesota Press.

Blackburn, Simon (1994) *Oxford Dictionary of Philosophy*, Oxford and New York: Oxford University Press.

Bourdieu, Pierre (1988) *Homo Academicus*, trans. Peter Collier, Cambridge: Polity Press.

Brecht, Bertolt (1962) *Mother Courage and her Children. A Chronicle of the Thirty Years War*, trans. Eric Bentley, London: Methuen.

Brown, Andrew (1992) *Roland Barthes: The Figures of Writing*, Oxford: Clarendon Press.

Burgin, Victor (1996) *In/Different Spaces: Place and Memory in Visual Culture*, Berkeley, Los Angeles and London: University of California Press.

—— (1997) 'Barthes's Discretion', in Jean-Michael Rabaté (ed.) *Writing the Image After Roland Barthes*, Philadelphia: University of Pennsylvania Press, 19–31.

Calvet, Louis-Jean (1994) *Roland Barthes: A Biography*, trans. Sarah Wykes, Oxford: Polity Press.

Camus, Albert (1975) *The Myth of Sisyphus*, Harmondsworth: Penguin.

—— (2000) *The Outsider*, Harmondsworth: Penguin.

Champagne, Roland (1984) *Literary History in the Wake of Roland Barthes: Redefining the Myths of Reading*, Birmingham, Alabama: Summa Publications.

Cuddon, J. A. (1991) *Dictionary of Literary Terms and Literary Theory*, Harmondsworth: Penguin.

Culler, Jonathan (2002) *Roland Barthes: A Very Short Introduction*, Oxford: Oxford University Press.

Derrida, Jacques (1973) *Speech and Phenomenon and Other Essays on Husserl's Theory of Signs*, trans. David B. Allison, Evanston: Northwestern University Press.

—— (1976) *Of Grammatology*, trans. Gayatri Chakravorty Spivak, Baltimore and London: The Johns Hopkins University Press.

—— (1981) *Writing and Difference*, trans. Allan Bass, London: Routledge and Kegan Paul.

—— (2001) 'The Deaths of Roland Barthes', in Pascale-Anne Brault and Michael Naas (eds) *The Work of Mourning*, Chicago and London: The University of Chicago Press, 31–67.

ffrench, Patrick (1995) *The Time of Theory: A History of 'Tel Quel'*, Oxford: Clarendon Press.

——— and Roland-François Lack (eds) (1998) *The 'Tel Quel' Reader*, London and New York: Routledge.

Foucault, Michel (1979) 'What is an Author?' in José V. Harari (ed.) *Textual Strategies: Perspectives in Post-Structuralist Criticism*, New York: Cornell University Press, 141–60.

Freedman, Sanford and Carole Anne Taylor (1983) *Roland Barthes: A Bibliographical Reader's Guide*, New York and London: Garland.

Grosz, Elizabeth (1990) *Jacques Lacan: A Feminist Introduction*, London and New York: Routledge.

Hawthorn, Jeremy (1992) *A Concise Glossary of Contemporary Literary Theory*, London and New York: Edward Arnold.

Jefferson, Ann and David Robey (1986) *Modern Literary Theory: A Comparative Introduction*, London: B.T. Batsford.

Knight, Diana (1997a) *Barthes and Utopia: Space, Travel, Writing*, Oxford: Clarendon Press.

——— (1997b) 'Roland Barthes, or The Woman Without a Shadow' in Jean-Michael Rabaté (ed.) *Writing the Image After Roland Barthes*, Philadelphia: University of Pennsylvania Press, 132–43.

——— (ed.) (2000) *Critical Essays on Roland Barthes*, New York: G.K. Hall.

Kristeva, Julia (1980) *Desire in Language: A Semiotic Approach to Literature and Art*, ed. Leon S. Roudiez, trans. Thomas Gora, Alice Jardine and Leon S. Roudiez, New York: Columbia State University Press.

——— (1984) *Revolution in Poetic Language*, trans. Margaret Waller, New York: Columbia University Press.

——— (2000) 'Barthes's Voice' in Diana Knight (ed.) *Critical Essays on Roland Barthes*, New York: G.K. Hall, 138–41.

Lacan, Jacques (1989) *Écrits: A Selection*, trans. Alan Sheridan, London: Tavistock/Routledge.

Landow, George P. (1992) *Hypertext: The Convergence of Contemporary Critical Theory and Technology*, Baltimore and London: The Johns Hopkins University Press.

—— (ed.) (1994) *Hyper/Text/Theory*, Baltimore and London: The Johns Hopkins University Press.

Langiulli, Nino (ed.) (1997) *European Existentialism*, New Brunswick and London: Transaction Pubs.

Lavers, Annette (1982) *Roland Barthes: Structuralism and After*, London: Methuen.

Lévi-Strauss, Claude (1966) *The Savage Mind*, London: Weidenfield & Nicolson.

—— (1968) *Structural Anthropology*, trans. Claire Jacobson and Brooke Grundfest Schoepf, Harmondsworth: Penguin.

—— (1992) *The Raw and the Cooked. Introduction to a Science of Mythology: 1*, trans. John and Doreen Weightman, Harmondsworth: Penguin.

Lombardo, Patrizia (1989) *The Three Paradoxes of Roland Barthes*, Athens and London: The University of Georgia Press.

MacCabe, Colin (1997) 'Barthes and Bazin: The Ontology of the Image', in Jean-Michael Rabaté (ed.) *Writing the Image After Roland Barthes*, Philadelphia: University of Pennsylvania Press, 71–6.

Macksey, Richard and Eugenio Donato (eds) (1972) *The Structuralist Controversy: The Languages and the Sciences of Man*, Baltimore and London: The Johns Hopkins University Press.

McGraw, Betty R. and Steven Ungar (eds) (1989) *Signs in Culture: Roland Barthes Today*, Iowa: University of Iowa Press.

Miller, D. A. (1992) *Bringing Out Roland Barthes*, Berkeley: University of California Press.

Miller, Nancy K. (1988) *Subject to Change: Reading Feminist Writing*, New York: Columbia University Press.

Moriarty, Michael (1991) *Roland Barthes*, Oxford: Polity Press.

Mortimer, Armine Kotin (1989) *The Gentlest Law: Roland Barthes's 'The Pleasure of the Text'*, New York: Peter Lang.

Perloff, Marjorie (1997) '"What has occurred only once": Barthes's Winter Garden/Boltanski's Archives of the Dead' in Jean-Michael

Rabaté (ed.) *Writing the Image After Roland Barthes*, Philadelphia: University of Pennsylvania Press, 32–58.

Picard, Ramond (1969) *New Criticism or New Fraud?*, trans. Frank Towne, Pullman: Washington State University Press.

Propp, Vladimir (1984) *Theory and History of Folklore*, ed. Anatoly Liberman, trans. Ariadna Y. Martin and Richard P. Martin, Manchester: Manchester University Press.

Rabaté, Jean-Michel (ed.) (1997) *Writing the Image After Roland Barthes*, Philadelphia: University of Pennsylvania Press.

Ribière, Mireille (2002) *Barthes: A Beginner's Guide*, London: Hodder & Stoughton.

Robbe-Grillet, Alain (1960) *Jealousy*, trans. Richard Howard, London: John Calder.

Ross, Kristin (1995) *Fast Cars, Clean Bodies: Decolonization and the Reordering of French Culture*, Cambridge, Mass. and London: The MIT Press.

Rylance, Rick (1994) *Roland Barthes*, Modern Critical Theorists, Hemel Hempstead: Havester Wheatsheaf.

Sartre, Jean-Paul (1956) *Being and Nothingness: An Essay on Phenomenological Ontology*, trans. Hazel E. Barnes, New York: Philosophical Library.

—— (2001) *What is Literature?*, trans. Bernard Frechtman, intro. David Chute, London: Routledge.

Saussure, Ferdinand de (1974) *Course in General Linguistics*, ed. Charles Bally, Albert Sechehaye in collaboration with Albert Reidlinger, trans. Wade Baskin, London: Fontana.

Shawcross, Nancy M. (1997) *Roland Barthes and Photography: The Critical Tradition in Perspective*, Gainsville: University Press of Florida.

Sollers, Philippe (1986) *Event, with an Essay by Roland Barthes*, trans. Bruce Benderson and Ursule Molinaro, New York: Red Dust.

Solomon, Robert C. (1988) *Continental Philosophy Since 1750: The Rise and Fall of the Self*, New York and Oxford: Oxford University Press.

Stafford, Andy (1998) *Roland Barthes: Phenomenon and Myth: An Intellectual Biography*, Edinburgh: Edinburgh University Press.

Thody, Philip (1977) *Roland Barthes: A Conservative Estimate*, London: Macmillan.

Todorov, Tzvetan (2000) 'Late Barthes', in Diana Knight (ed.) *Critical Essays on Roland Barthes*, New York: G.K. Hall, 123–8.

Tuman, Myron C. (ed.) (1992) *Literacy Online: The Promise [and Peril] of Reading and Writing with Computers*, Pittsburgh and London: University of Pittsburgh Press.

Ungar, Steven (1983) *Roland Barthes: The Professor of Desire*, Lincoln and London: University of Nebraska Press.

Wiseman, Mary Bittner (1989) *The Ecstasies of Roland Barthes*, London and New York: Routledge.

INDEX

Adorno, Theodor 19
Algeria 10, 36
Allen, Graham 81, 82
Althusser, Louis 75, 105
'Astrologie' 142
'At Le Palace Tonight . . .' 149
Atopia 103–4
Attridge, Derek 126
avant-garde, the 28–31, 45, 143;
    assimilation of 108; and Barthes
    26; and the bourgeoisie 139; and
    commitment 13–14; and
    criticism 53, 54; and literature
    88, 103, 106, 123

Bakhtin, Mikhail 79–81
Balzac, Honore de 84, 87, 88, 90,
    91, 93, 104, 106, 144
Barthes, Alice 2
Barthes, Berthe 2
Barthes, Henriette (née Binger)
    1–2, 125–9, 131, 132, 134,
    147
Barthes, Louis 1–2

Barthes, Roland passim; amateur
    musician 2, 6, 116; career 2–3,
    53, 79; childhood 1; cinema 115,
    122; Collège de France 2, 3;
    computer technology 136; death
    of 134–5; École Prâtique des
    Hautes Études 2, 54, 56; and
    fashion 1, 38, 46–52, 56, 57;
    and the filmic 122–3;
    homosexuality 5, 98–9, 106,
    107, 138, 149, 151; and Japan
    70–3, 75, 77, 144; and the
    media 1, 34, 46, 49, 120–1,
    136; and music 2, 6, 115–18,
    124, 148; plans to write a novel
    108; Sorbonne 2; and theatre 5,
    27, 28–30, 31, 38, 142, 143;
    tuberculosis 2, 26
Barthes: Selected Writings 148
Bataille, Georges 75
Battleship Potemkin 122
Baudrillard, Jean 63
Being and Nothingness 11
Benderson, Bruce 147

Bensmaïa, Réda 149
'Bichon and the Blacks' 35
Blackburn, Simon 12, 157
'Blind and Dumb Criticism' 55
bliss (jouissance) 101–7, 122, 123, 145
'Blue Guide, The' 35
Boltanski, Christian 130
Bourdieu, Pierre 54
bourgeoisie 12, 66; and assimilation 19–20, 22, 24, 34, 85, 141; and criticism 55; culture of 34–6, 38, 39, 72, 96, 100, 101, 139; ideology of 44, 52; and Literature 30–1; 59, 61; and Michelet 26; and reading 116; rise of 12–13; theatre 28–9, 142, 143; writer 18, 31
Brecht, Bertolt 28–9, 31, 143
Bringing Out Roland Barthes 138
Brown, Andrew 150
'Buffet Finishes Off New York' 142
Burgin, Victor 122

Calvet, Louis-Jean 2, 3, 29, 54, 134, 135
Camera Lucida 4, 5, 115, 124, 125–32, 134–5, 147
Camus, Albert 11, 19–20, 21, 22, 141
Camus, Renaud 98–9
Champagne, Roland 150
'Change the Object Itself: Mythology Today' 65–6
Chateaubriand, François Auguste René, Vicomte de 145
Citröen D.S. 34
Clark, Robert 154
codes (cultural, hermeneutic, proairetic, semic, symbolic) 86–8

commitment 5, 24, 25, 31, 103, 143; Sartre's idea of 10, 12–14; and *Writing Degree Zero* 15–17, 141
Communications 45, 143
Compagnon, Antoine 151
connotation 49–51, 65, 71, 89, 119, 120, 121, 122, 123
'Cottage Industry' 142
Course in General Linguistics 39
Coverdale, Linda 147
Critical Essays 29, 143
Criticism and Truth 54–6, 61, 62, 64, 143
Critique 147
Cuddon, J.A. 13, 71, 158
Culler, Jonathan 45, 150
cultural studies 1, 73, 135

Dadaism 13
'Death of the Author, The' 1, 4, 60–1, 73–6, 77, 135, 138, 148; and intertextuality 81; and *Roland Barthes by Roland Barthes* 146; and theory of the text 82–3
'Deaths of Roland Barthes, The' 128, 139
de Beauvoir, Simone 11
deconstruction 66, 67–8, 70, 72, 74, 106, 144
denotation 49–51, 65, 71, 119, 120, 121
Derrida, Jacques 63, 67–70, 71, 74, 75, 77, 79, 139; and *Camera Lucida* 128; and *Tel Quel* 75
De Gaulle, Charles 63
de Sade, Marquis 64, 144
de Saussure, Ferdinand 119; and Bakhtin 80; Derrida on 67–8; linguistic theories of 39–41, 56–7; and semiology 45–6
dialectic 22–3, 31, 96

dialogism 79, 80–1
différance 70
'Dining Car' 142
'Division of Language, The' 97
Dominici, Gaston 35
'Dominici, or The Triumph of
    Literature' 35
Donota, Eugenio 67
double-voiced discourse 80
doxa 117; doxa/paradoxa opposition
    95–100; endoxal logic 89–90; and
    orthodox language 101
Drame 90, 91–2, 147

Eiffel Tower and Other Mythologies, The
    142
Eiffel Tower, The 38
'Eiffel Tower, The' 142
Einstein, Albert 34, 137
Eisenstein, Sergei 122, 123, 126
Elements of Semiology 45–6, 60, 143
Elle 37, 46
Empire of Signs 70–3, 77, 89, 98,
    130, 144
Engels, Friedrich 12, 23
Event 147
Existentialism 9, 10–11, 14, 54, 55,
    144

Fashion System, The 46–52, 60, 64,
    71, 72, 77, 98, 119, 135, 139,
    143
Fedkiew, Pat 149
ffrench, Patrick 75
Fischer-Dieskau, Dietrich 116–17
Flaubert, Gustave 19, 20, 104, 145
'Flaubert and the Sentence' 145
Fleming, Ian 58
Foucault, Michel 3, 63, 74, 75
Fourier, Charles 64, 144
France-Dimanche 66
Frankfurt School, The 19

Freedman, Sanford 150
Freud, Sigmund 105, 137
'From Work to Text' 82–3, 88, 148

Goldfinger 58
Graham, Billy 34, 35
Grain of the Voice, The 147
grain of the voice, the 117, 124
'Great Family of Man, The' 37
Greimas, A.J. 59
Grosz, Elizabeth 110

haiku, 71
Hawthorn, Jeremy 105
Heath, Stephen 64, 146, 148
Hébert, Jacques 16, 17, 18
hedonism 5, 96, 100–8, 137, 145
Hegel, G. 23
heteroglossia 80–1
Hines, Lewis H. 126
Hitler, Adolf 11
Hjelmslev, Louis 50
Howard, Richard 141, 142, 143,
    144, 145, 146, 147, 148, 149,
    151
Hypertext 154

image-repertoire 109–12
'Image, The' 99, 139–40
Imaginary, the 109–12
Incidents 98, 149
'Incidents' 149
Image-Music-Text 65, 146, 148
'Inaugural Lecture, Collège de
    France' 3, 146–7
intertextuality 1, 5, 90, 91, 92,
    135; and A Lover's Discourse 109,
    112, 146; and the theory of the
    text 74, 79–83, 87–8, 93
'Introduction to the Structural
    Analysis of Narratives' 4–5,
    56–61, 77, 87, 149

Jakobson, Roman 106
Jefferson, Ann 57
Jesuit Order 64, 144
Johns Hopkins University 66–7

Keats, John 133
Keuneman, Katrine Pilcher 143
Klein, William 126
Knight, Diana 129, 149, 150–1
Kristeva, Julia 63, 136; and Bakhtin
    79, 81; and intertextuality 82,
    102; pheno-text and geno-text
    117–18; the semiotic and the
    symbolic 118; and *Tel Quel*
    75–6

Lacan, Jacques 105, 110, 118
Landow, George P. 136, 154
Langiulli, Nino 11, 160
language: acratic 97; encratic 97
Lanson, Gustave 54
Lavers, Annette 141, 142, 151
L'Arc 27
Le Figaro 148
Le Jardin des modes 46
Les Lettres nouvelles 33, 142, 148
L'Étranger (*The Outsider / The Stranger*)
    21, 22
Le Monde 148
Lévi-Strauss, Claude 60
Lexias 86, 87, 91
L'Express 37
Life of Rancé 145
L'Humanité 149
'Light of the Sud-Ouest, The' 149
L'Infini 75
*Literary Encyclopedia and Literary
    Dictionary* 154
Lombardo, Patrizia 151
Lover's Discourse, A 4, 95, 98,
    109–12, 125, 146
'Loving Schumann' 116

Loyola, Ignatius 64, 144
Lydon, Mary 151

MacCabe, Colin 139
Macksey, Richard 67
Mallarmé, Stephane 21
Marie-Claire 45
Marty, Eric 141
Marxism 12, 20, 23, 25, 99, 100,
    101, 105, 144; and Brecht 29;
    and Existentialism 14, 16, 141;
    Frankfurt School 19; and literary
    criticism 54–5, 84; and post-war
    France 14; and the subject 105
*Marxism and the Philosophy of
    Language* 80
Marx, Karl 12, 23
May 1968 (revolt) 63, 73
McGraw, Betty R. 151
Michelet 25–7, 31, 141–2, 145
Michelet, Jules 25–7, 29, 141–2
Miller, D.A. 138
Miller, Nancy K. 138, 151
Miller, Richard 144, 145
'Mirror-Stage, The' 110
Mitterand, François 134
Molinaro, Ursule 147
monoglossia 81
Montaigne, Michel Eyquem de 149
Moriarty, Michael 152
Mortimer, Armine Kotin 152
Mother Courage 29
'Musica Practica' 115
Myth of Sisyphus, The 19–20
Mythologies 4, 5, 26, 33–9, 55, 60,
    72, 98, 134, 135, 136, 142;
    assimilation of 65; and the Doxa
    96; and fashion 51; François
    Mitterand's enjoyment of 134;
    and photography 118–20; and
    semiology 42–5
'Myth Today' 39, 42–5, 46, 64

Nazi occupation of France 9
neutral, the 96–9, 101, 103,
  112, 126
New Critical Essays 145
New Criticism or New Fraud? 54,
  143
new historicism 27
nouveau roman 13, 28, 29–30,
  31
novelistic, the 108–12, 113, 125,
  146

Œuvres complètes 54, 141
On Racine 27–8, 54, 142
'Ornamental Cookery' 37
'Outcomes of the Text' 97

Panzera, Charles 116–17
paradigmatic (axis of language)
  57
Paris-Match 35, 37, 38, 45
Parti communiste français (PCF)
  14, 20
Perloff, Marjorie 130
photography 6, 37–8, 42, 44, 46,
  115, 117, 118–32, 147, 152–3;
  obtuse meaning of 123–4, 126;
  obvious meaning of 123, 126;
  punctum 125–8, 130, 131, 147;
  studium 125–8, 130, 131, 147
'Photographic Message, The' 118
'Plates of the Encyclopedia, The'
  145
Picard, Raymond 54, 55, 143
Plato 66, 105
Playboy 148
pleasure (plaisir) 96, 100–8, 116,
  123, 145
Pleasure of the Text, The 95, 100–8,
  116, 122, 124, 145, 152
'Poujade and the Intellectuals' 35
Poujade, Pierre 35

post-structuralism 1, 5, 51, 63, 77,
  101, 143, 144, 147, 153; and
  'The Death of the Author' 73–4;
  and Derrida 67, 70; and history
  27; and the subject 105–6; and
  Tel Quel 74, 75; text and
  intertextuality 79–93; and
  writing (écriture) 15, 17, 72
Propp, Vladimir 58–9
'Proust and Names' 145
Proust, Marcel 104, 108
psychoanalysis 1, 99; and the image-
  repertoire 109; and psychoanalytical literary criticism 28,
  54, 142; and the subject 105, 118

Queen Mother, the (UK) 38, 43

Rabaté, Jean-Michel 122, 152
Racine, Jean 27–8, 29, 31, 142
Raw and the Cooked, The 60
realism 31, 86, 89, 90, 120; and
  bourgeois theatre 29; and
  Brechtian theatre 28–30; critique
  of 20–1; and the structural
  analysis of narratives 59–60
'Reality Effect, The' 5, 20
referent, the 119–24, 129, 130
Renault 45
Responsibility of Forms, The 148
'Rhetoric of the Image, The' 5, 118,
  120, 121
Ribière, Mireille 152
Robbe-Grillet, Alain 28, 29–30,
  90
Robey, David 57
Rochefoucauld, François de
  Marsillac, La 145
Roland Barthes by Roland Barthes
  95–100, 101, 106–7, 108–9,
  125, 145–6
'Romans in Films, The' 35

Rustle of Language, The 148
Rylance, Rick 52, 152

Sade/Fourier/Loyola 64–5, 144
Sarrasine 84–9, 103, 106, 144
Sartre, Jean-Paul 9, 10–14, 15, 16,
    18, 19, 20, 24, 26, 135, 141
Savage Mind, The 60
Schumann, Robert Alexander 116
semiology 1, 5, 33–52, 53, 62, 99,
    142, 143, 144, 146, 148–9; and
    deconstruction 70; in the EPHE
    54; and Japan 70–3; and the
    photographic image 118–24; and
    post-structuralism 64–6
Semiotic Challenge, The 84, 148
semiotics 39, 77, 89, 111, 153
Shakespeare, William 28, 133
Shawcross, Nancy 126, 152–3
sign (signifier, signified) destruction
    of 65–6, 79, 93; the empty sign
    70–3, 77; equivalence between
    signifier and signified 42–3, 49,
    51; and intertextuality 83; lack of
    stable signified 88–90, 100, 116;
    and *A Lover's Discourse* 111; and
    photography 123–4, 126; in
    Saussurean linguistics 40–1, 119;
    and semiology 45–6, 143;
    signification (second-order
    meaning) 43–4; transcendental
    signified 67–70; and writing
    (écriture) 75–6, 77, 95, 131–2
signifiance 83–4, 87, 93, 106,
    116–17, 122, 123, 124, 126, 145
Smith, Colin 141, 143
'Soap-Powders and Detergents'
    35–6
'Sociology and Socio-Logic' 60
Socrates 23
'Soirées de Paris' 149
Solomon, Robert C. 11, 161

Sontag, Susan 141, 143, 148
Sorbonne 2, 63
Sollers, Philippe 63, 75, 90, 91–2,
    93, 103, 106, 147
Sollers Writer 90, 91–2, 97, 147
Speech Genres 80
speech and language (parole and
    langue) 40, 56, 67, 80, 83
Speech and Phenomenon 66
Spiritual Exercises, The 64
Stafford, Andy 45, 153
Structural Anthropology 60
structuralism 1, 5, 15, 17, 27, 33,
    51, 53–62, 93, 142, 143, 153;
    and 'Death of the Author' 74,
    82, 138; and deconstruction 70;
    movement beyond 65–6, 96, 99,
    108; and post-structuralism
    66–7, 77; and *Sade/Fourier/Loyola*
    64; and Saussurean linguistics
    39–41; structural analysis of
    narratives 52, 79, 84, 87, 136,
    144, 149; and the subject 105;
    and *Tel Quel* 75
'Structure, Sign and Play within the
    Discourse of the Human Sciences'
    67–70
subject, the 75, 105, 107, 118
Surrealism 13
Symbolism 13
syntagmatic (axis of language) 57,
    88
S/Z 79, 84–9, 91, 92, 93, 98, 102,
    108, 115, 122, 144

Tales of Parisian Life 84
Taylor, Carole Anne 150
text 75, 77, 79–93, 135; and bliss
    (jouissance) 101–7, 117, 122,
    123, 145; and computer
    technologies 136; geno-text
    117–18; novelistic text 112; as

opposed to the work 76;
pheno-text 117–18; and pleasure
(plaisir) 96, 100–8, 116, 123,
145; readerly text 88–92, 93,
103, 122, 126; textual analysis
83–8, 138, 149; theory of 74,
79–83, 93, 96, 102, 122;
writerly text 88–92, 93, 103,
115, 122, 126, 136, 145
Tel Quel 15, 26, 74, 75, 90, 144,
148
'Theory of the Text' 82–3, 84
'There is No Robbe-Grillet School'
30
'Third Meaning, The' 5, 122,
126
Thody, Philip 147, 153
Todorov, Tzvetan 134, 136
Tokyo 72
Tour de France 34
Tricks 98–9
Tuman, Myron C. 136
'Two Salons, The' 142

Ungar, Steven 151, 153

Valéry, Paul 43
Van Der Zee, James 126
Vichy Government 9
Vietnam War 63

Ward, Matthew 143
'War of Languages, The' 97
Wessing, Koen 126
'What is an Author?' 74
What is Literature? 10–14, 18, 141
'Whose Theatre? Whose *Avant-
Garde?*' 30
Wiseman, Mary Bittner 153
'Writers, Intellectuals, Teachers'
140
Writing and Difference 66
Writing Degree Zero 5, 9–24, 25–6,
30, 31, 34, 39, 45, 59, 72, 107,
108, 141, 143, 145
writing (écriture) 25, 131–2, 136,
145; acculturation of 65; and
commitment 26, 31, 140, 141,
143; contrasted to écrivance 97;
contrasted with language and
style 14–18, 27, 141; cultural
writing 89, 91; and Japan 72–3,
75; and Literature 24, 31, 141;
opposed to the Doxa 100–1, 113,
140; and play of meaning 70;
post-structuralist idea of 75–6,
95, 97, 101; the writerly 88, 90,
115; zero degree writing 21–2,
141

Zupko, Sarah 153–4